FIRST STEPS TOGETHER

FIRST STEPS TOGETHER:

Home-school early literacy in European contexts

Edited by Henrietta Dombey and Margaret Meek Spencer

Trentham Books/IEDPE

First published in 1994 by Trentham Books Limited

Trentham Books Limited
Westview House
734 London Road
Oakhill
Stoke-on-Trent
Staffordshire
England ST4 5NP

British Library Cataloguing Publication Data
A catalogue record for this book is available from the British Library.

ISBN: 1 85856 001 2

Designed and Typeset by Trentham Print Design Limited, Chester
and printed by BPC Wheatons Limited, Exeter.

CONTENTS

Notes on Contibutors

Florence Beetlestone specialises in early childhood education in the School of Primary and Secondary Education at the University of Greenwich where she teaches on initial and in-service teacher education courses.

Jean Biarnès works at the Université Paris XIII where he directs a number of projects involving both research and teacher education attacking the problems of economic, social and cultural exclusion in the countries of northern industrialised Europe. The group's action research is focused on preventing school dropout and on working directly with those already excluded from formal education.

Henrietta Dombey works in the School of Education at the University of Brighton, where she teaches both students in initial teacher education and teachers on in-service courses. In her teaching and in her own research her focus is on early literacy learning.

Maria Luisa Gil is a Nursery Teacher currently working as an Nursery Advisor in the district of Palencia, Spain.

Eve Gregory works in the Faculty of Education at Goldsmiths' College, University of London, where she teaches on initial teacher education, in-service and advanced degree courses. Her teaching and her own research focus on early literacy and children from linguistic and cultural minorities.

Esperanza Pilar Gutièrrez is a Nursery Teacher in the primary school of Nuestra Señora del Villar in Laguna de Duero in central

Spain. She is currently the area coordinator of the Athene and Mercury projects which are introducing new technology into nursery schools. She also contributes to programmes of in-service education at the Teachers' Centre.

Roger Hancock works in the London boroughs of Tower Hamlets and Hackney where he co-ordinates projects to increase understanding and collaboration between home and school.

Peter Hannon teaches and researches in the Division of Education at the University of Sheffield in the north of England. He directed the Sheffield Early Literacy Development Project and has interests in literacy, home-school relations and early childhood education.

Helen James is Deputy Headteacher at Bangabandhu Primary School in the London Borough of Tower Hamlets. She was previously an Advisory Teacher at the Centre for Language in Primary Education, London.

Calliope Kyrdi is a Museum Educator with a special interest in supporting early literacy learning through parental involvement, museum and environmental education.

Margaret Meek is Emeritus Reader at the University of London Institute of Education where she supervises research students. Her concerns are children learning to read and write and the literature texts that are part of that learning.

Maria Paz Ortega is a Nursery Teacher in a rural school in Astudillo, Palencia Province, where she works with children from 3 to 6 years.

Maria Pilar Retuerto works as a Nursery and Early Primary Teacher in a rural school in San Cébrian de Campos in Palencia Province, with children aged from 3 to 8 years.

Geoff Sheath teaches in the School of Primary and Secondary Education at the University of Greenwich. He has a particular interest in establishing co-operation between home and school in mathematics education.

Aris Sioutis is a primary school teacher in the area of Vyronas in Athens, and is particularly interested in developing literacy through environmental education and action.

Penny Smith works in the School of Primary and Secondary Education at the University of Greenwich, where she teaches students in initial teacher education and teachers on in-service courses. Her particular interest lies in the development of literacy in young children.

J Lino Barrio Valencia teaches in the Departamento de Didáctica de la Lengua y la Literatura at the University of Valladolid, in central Spain, where he works in initial and in-service teacher education. He has completed a number of action research projects and is currently investigating the use of computers in nursery education.

Jo Weinberger is completing a longitudinal study at the University of Sheffield into the effects of children's early experiences of literacy at home. A former nursery teacher, she worked with Peter Hannon on the Sheffield Early Literacy Development Project.

Margaret Wyeth is Headteacher at Gallions Mount Primary School in the London Borough of Greenwich. She has been a teacher in London for over 20 years.

INTRODUCTION

Avant Propos

This book is one of the first fruits of IEDPE, the European Institute for the Development of the Potential of All Children. It marks a new beginning in collaboration by teachers and researchers who, in different European countries with their diverse histories and cultures, have a care and responsibility for the early stages of children's reading and writing in communities where literacy is seen as a necessary part of citizenship.

The common theme of these chapters is the experience shared by all children: the move they make when they go from the domestic familiarity of home to the social world of school. At home, in the company of their family, caregivers and neighbours, children learn to speak their mother tongue. In doing so they learn their culture: 'the way we do things and talk about them'. School is both the society of children and the place of official instruction and institutionalised learning. Children's entry into the world of written language spans this transition.

From the diversity of cultural and social practices which are the background to the events recorded in these pages there emerge common concerns about children's first steps in learning to read and write, and the views which children, their parents and their teachers have of these enterprises. By bringing these descriptive instances together we have discovered that we share certain theoretical concerns and pedagogical practices. Also the teachers who report their work offer to their readers, and to each other, new insights and new strategies.

Of particular importance is the general emphasis on the relations and interactions between parents and teachers. Recent research in many countries makes it clear, and these vignettes confirm, that positive attitudes to learning to read, the pleasure that encourages beginners to persist in their efforts to be successful are formed, and can be supported, before children are formally taught in school. In a variety of settings where children are the focus of adult attention we see the unfolding of new kinds of partnerships.

In some instances, the teachers visit the homes of the children. With consummate tact and openness they show their genuine desire to negotiate shared understanding of the place and practices of literacy in everyday family life. At other times, parents join the teachers and the children at school where reading lessons become less of a mystery. What readers do is part of the enlarged understanding right from the start. In these conditions teachers can make better provisions for reading and writing, and parents are reassured that their children can learn important lessons at home *and* at school. Then everybody, parents, teachers and children, learns to ask 'the good questions' about literacy, its nature and functions.

Although the teachers who have written these pages have drawn widely on their knowledge of work in research they have not presented the findings as formal research papers. This is not an exercise in comparative education. Instead, we see how teachers watch what children do: the kinds of thinking that teachers engage in as they respond to different literate activities. We can now see some clear outcomes. First, the continuing confirmation that reading and writing are functions of language, linked to the other functions, speaking and listening. Then we become aware of the overarching importance of bilingualism. This reminds us that European frontiers will soon be open conduits for languages and literacies. Also, we see that what begins as social conversation about books and stories leads children and adults to the interior dialogues of individual readers and writers.

A particular attraction of this collection is the variety of contexts in which collaborative teaching and learning go on. Without premeditation, our colleagues have discovered that their work in different institutions has a common emphasis on the initiatives taken by the children to interpret meanings from texts. Reading emerges from these pages as a predominantly social activity. On this fact rests the internationality of this book as an undertaking and the essential rightness of the IEDPE emphasis on the potential of *all* children. Even if the children of Sheffield, Palencia, London and Athens have yet to discover each other as Europeans, their teachers have a vision of their literacy as something which will go beyond the locality of their learning to read and write.

No European city is monocultural nor monolingual. Children whose mother tongue is not that of the dominant culture where they live are more numerous in many inner city schools than at any other time in our common history. Although the children pictured here have particular linguistic hurdles to surmount, they share, more deeply, the commonality of 'the stranger'. The problem for their teachers is, not how to deal with the techniques of reading instruction, but how to understand the cultural assumptions that lie behind what children do and the questions they ask. In different ways evidence of this emerges from all the close observations presented here. It is particularly clear in the case of Tony and Jean-Francois in Chapter 2. It also underlies the insights of teachers who know the dangers of unexamined beliefs about the behaviour of 'other people'. In this collaborative presentation we anticipate how the informing ideas of IEDPE may continue to be shaped and extended.

As an accomplishment, literacy is very complex. Descriptions of it must, at all times, include the social contexts of the learners, their interactions with adults who help them, and with the texts in the local situations where their learning begins. As they come to be engaged in the literate practices of their culture — what others around them do with reading and writing — children learn to use reading to shape their own intentions, to ask questions about the world, and to move into the modern networks of communications as well as into the stories and literature of the past. In Europe, as elsewhere, the world comes to children in books as a series of possible quests and explorations. Although television has taken over some of this function, it cannot replace reading as a distinctive experience; the change of consciousness described as being 'lost in a book'. Nor can modern electronic systems replace the 'handiness' (i.e. in the hand) of books as sources of information. The first steps in literacy do not remain local for long. Books as windows on the world soon enlarge children's horizons. We count on them to cross the frontiers of international understanding, not only in education, but in whatever other spheres of concern we share. Stories are composed of language and the imagination of the teller. Yet they encompass the world and create new possibilities for all.

We hope that the principled pedagogic practices detailed here will help children in Europe and elsewhere to read both texts and the world. From these modest beginnings we intend to go on to wider and deeper understandings of what happens when children enter the domain of the written word. We have not weighed down this modest first step with the ritual criticisms to which most of us are accustomed; the short book lists cover the most relevant sources. We warmly welcome the advice of anyone who would care to contribute to the extension of this enterprise.

Henrietta Dombey
Margaret Meek

The European Community Action Research Programme funded a number of projects concerned with the prevention of illiteracy in the community's member states. Their purpose was to collect and compare practical initiatives taken by teachers and parents to support children's earliest encounters with writing. What follows are the details of one such project in Sheffield, England. In England, most children go to school officially in the year of their fifth birthday. Before then, some go to nursery schools, but there is no general official provision for this. Most parents want their children to learn to read as soon as possible but do not always realise that everyday activities contain many literacy lessons which do not need to be explicitly taught. The writers of this chapter visited families at home, with the intention of making parents aware of how children read print in the environment and to promote parents' understanding of the nature of this awareness. From this experience we can see the need for well-designed follow-up studies to assess the effect of early intervention on children's later development in literacy.

Chapter 1

SHARING NEW IDEAS ABOUT PRE-SCHOOL LITERACY WITH PARENTS

Peter Hannon and Jo Weinberger

In Sheffield we have been trying some new ways of working with parents to promote children's literacy development before they enter school. Here we describe what has been done in the *Sheffield Early Literacy Development Project*, explain some ideas behind it, and share what we have learnt from our work with parents.

Sheffield is a large industrial city in the north of England. The project was a collaboration between the University of Sheffield and the City Education Department. Together with a colleague from the city, Cathy Nutbrown, we worked on the project from 1988 to 1990. Although it was not a large-scale project (it was primarily a research study and the original work was carried out with a group of families with 20 pre-school children), many of our methods seem to have been taken up in other parts of the UK.

We tried two main methods — *home visiting* and *parent meetings*. More details of these can be found in the booklet, *Ways of Working with Parents to Promote Early Literacy Development*, listed at the end of the chapter.

Home Visiting

We have visited pre-school children and parents at home in order to introduce resources for literacy into the home, model ways of using them, and to share ideas about early literacy development with parents. Members of the project team — each with experience as a pre-school teacher, carried out the visiting. Visits lasted between half an hour and an hour and have included activities such as sharing books, talking about early writing, and identifying print in the environment.

Visiting was carried out in as flexible a way as possible in order to respond to the individual needs of families but there was some structure in that they usually had the format of a *review*, some *input* and a *plan*.

Review: Visits usually began by looking back at what parents and children had been doing since the previous visit. Visitors asked parents for their views about any activities which had been suggested for the period between visits. We left books, paper and notebooks. We also suggested other activities, e.g. making small books together, cutting out pictures from magazines and labelling them, making a note of any print or logos the child was recognising, and sending us a letter.

Figure 1: Working with parents at home. Photograph by Frank Herrmann.

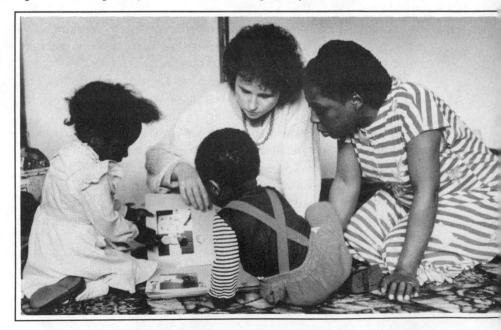

Input : Each visitor used slightly different resources but they usually included:

books suited to children's ages and interest
resources for mark making
examples of environmental print.

We were careful not to take in anything too unusual. We wanted what we did as far as possible to be part of the families' everyday life.

We had a range of children's books, mostly paperback, which we took into homes and which parents could borrow. In a visit at the start of the project, the children were given a folder with a pencil, pencil sharpener, plain paper and a lined notebook. In the visits, we used resources such as crayons, felt tips, glue pens and scissors, paper and envelopes, old Christmas cards and magazines. We also took photographs, some of which were used by the children to make their own books.

Plan: At the end of each visit we talked with the parents about the activities which we could leave for them to do, discussed their significance for literacy development, and arranged the next visit. We asked parents to save children's drawings or writing in a scrapbook, and if possible, to note the date and add comments.

Meetings for Parents

Parents were invited to a series of five meetings held in school. At the first, they worked with their own child on a variety of literacy-related activities. On subsequent occasions, a creche was provided to enable the parents to take part in the discussions and other activities without children. One meeting took place in a local public library.

In meetings parents received information about various aspects of literacy, for example, books and articles were shown and copies of relevant extracts circulated. Slides of print in the local environment demonstrated to parents the wealth of print that their children saw every day, and alerted them to some of the things their children were already able to read. Overhead transparencies of children's work illustrated children's increasing understanding and mastery of writing. A bookclub was available for parents to buy books if they wished, and books were also available for families to borrow.

But there had to be dialogue. Observations about children's literacy were shared. Parents were invited to show one another examples of their own children's writing, saved in scrapbooks, and to comment on what they noticed. There were opportunities to exchange ideas.

One activity that proved very successful was giving parents a jigsaw to complete which showed them their own child's stage of development in literacy. After each meeting a hand-out was devised that summarised what had happened, and included quotations and illustrations from all the families taking part.

Research Background

The ideas behind the Sheffield Project came from the idea of *emergent literacy* — a view of young children's literacy development which emphasises how children actively make meaning in their encounters with written language, andfocuses on what even the youngest children *can* do rather than what they *cannot* do.

The project tried to share these ideas with parents by concentrating on three strands of preschool literacy experiences — environmental print, early writing, and sharing books. We tried to show parents that they could influence their children's experience and learning by providing a model of literacy in relation to these three

Figure 2 Working with parents in a meeting. Photograph by Frank Herrmann.

Figure 3. The Jigsaw

strands, as well as providing opportunities for children, and recognising early achievements in their reading and writing.

The project was part of the European Commission Action Research Programme in the Prevention of Illiteracy and was linked to other projects in each of the 12 member states.

We evaluated the project by noting observations of children and parents, interviewing parents, collecting examples of children's mark-making and writing, and reflecting on our own experience as we worked with families.

More information about the rationale for the project and details about the research can be found in the report by Hannon, Weinberger and Nutbrown (1991) listed at the end of the chapter.

The Parents' Reaction

During the project we noted parents' reactions to our attempts to share ideas with them, and at the end an independent interviewer also sought their views. Here are some of their comments about *home visits*.

> 'Before you came I never thought about her reading things like mugs and boxes and signs and things. We read all sorts now from the top of the bus.'

> 'We found it difficult to know what books to pick for him. It's marvellous with you bringing books now. He's tending to want to sit and read a book now.

> 'He couldn't wait for you to come'.

> 'I've enjoyed today.'

> 'He's drawing more, and saying what it is. Like he drew a bottle in the pictures he sent you, and it looked like one.'

> 'It's given me a push .... I do more with him now.'

Comments about *meetings* included the following.

> 'I wouldn't have noticed so much without coming here'.

> 'I've really learned — and enjoyed it'.

> 'It's made me see more in children that I've never seen before. If if wasn't for the project I wouldn't have thought so clearly what children can do under the age of three'.

> 'I got a surprise when filling in the jigsaw bit. It surprised me how much he could do. There was only one blank' .

Figure 4: Three strands in early literacy experience.
a) Sharing books b) Emergent writing c) Environmental print

Photograph by Frank Herrmann.

Some Questions about our Work with Parents

Is it possible to work with parents on their children's literacy development?

Our experience here was very encouraging. Parents in our project were not self-selected or special in any way. They simply lived close to the school where the project was based and had children in the target age range (2 to 3). Parents were asked if they would be interested in taking part — and most were. We found that once they agreed to take part, none left the project, although several were in quite disadvantaged circumstances.

Despite many domestic difficulties no home visits were missed. Sometimes parents took the initiative in requesting changes of time or day. All parents attended some meetings in school (attendance overall averaged two thirds, the most common reason for non-attendance being child or family illness). It seems that, in a programme lasting up to six months, participation is not a problem.

More important, we found that our approach, based on emergent literacy, was experienced as meaningful by all parents or, as one mother put it, as 'an eye opener'.

On what family literacy does work with parents build?

As in other studies of early literacy, we found there was a significant amount of family literacy activity before the start of our project. All parents clearly valued literacy for their children. All children had access to some books (some had two or three, some had up to 50), and all children shared books at least sometimes with their parents. All the children had some opportunities and resources for drawing and writing.

However, conditions for the emergence of literacy were not equally favourable in all homes. Differences were particularly marked in terms of sharing books and having an adult model for literacy. Although about half the children had near daily experiences of book sharing, for a quarter of the children this happened once a week or less, and for some it was quite rare. All children saw their parent reading on occasions, but not all children saw parents writing. Only about a quarter of parents deliberately involved children in adult literacy activities such as writing a shopping list or checking TV programmes.

The message is that we can expect to find some literacy activities in virtually all homes, but it probably varies considerably in terms of quality and intensity.

What impact does this work have?

We found that our project was able to build on, and extend the literacy activities which were already taking place in the homes.

For families receiving home visits, there was a considerable increase in the number of times parents shared books with their children. We think this is probably because numerous good books were brought into homes and parents had the chance to observe and try out for themselves ways of sharing them with children. Some parents also recognised the significance of letting children take a more active role as they shared books together, encouraging them to handle the books themselves, turn over the pages, and talk about the pictures. Some parents began to provide more of a model in using literacy by writing in front of the children and by using the library.

Parents continued to provide for their children's drawing and writing, and in some cases extended the provision to include items such as forms and advertisement leaflets. Parents recognised more clearly their children's early writing attempts — demonstrated by their ability and development with the project team during home visits and readiness to discuss their children's work and its development with the project team during home visits and with other parents during meetings. During the project it became apparent that parents came to recognise how much sense their children could make of environmental print and were pointing it out to them more frequently.

The project also had an impact on family literacy. Some parents found that books borrowed through the project helped their own reading difficulties. Others started using the public library for themselves. Where there were older children in a family, they were almost always drawn into the project activities, and their teachers in school remarked on their increased interest in reading or writing. One parent summarised the influence of the project by saying, 'It's been a family thing.'

What difference does home visiting make?

As part of the research design, some of our families had more visits than others. We feel that home visiting probably does add to the effect of school-based work by the more frequent use of books, greater involvement of children when books are used, and an effect on older siblings.

We think there could be several reasons for this: time is given to one family, and the visitor's input can be geared specifically to their needs. Being visited at home by a professional clearly shows that the parents' role in their children's early literacy development is being taken very seriously. The parent (not the professional) has control of such things as the timing of the visit, where people sit, and who else is present. The children are somewhere familiar and the parent may feel less anxious about raising issues of concern to them. The family's own literacy materials can be incorporated easily into activities during the visit. The overall effect seemed to be to increase the parents' involvement and confidence and this in turn increased their capacity to engage in a dialogue.

Conclusions

We now know that the kind of work we have described is feasible and that it has some impact on pre-school children's literacy experience. That is an important finding which early childhood educators can use in their practice.

However, there are some further questions which need to be researched. For example, it would be interesting to know whether colleagues in other countries would find our approach valuable or even feasible. We also need to know how much difference it makes to children's literacy development (rather than just to their literacy experiences). To answer that question probably requires an experimental research design. We need to know what benefits can be expected if time and money is to be invested in activities such as home visiting. There is also the question of what training is needed to carry out this kind of work with parents.

Meanwhile we wish to give the last word to one of the parents in the Sheffield project.

> 'It's made me see more in children that I've never seen before. If it wasn't for the project I wouldn't have thought so clearly what children can do.'

Further information about the Project

Hannon, P., Weinberger, J. and A. Nutbrown, C. (1991) A study of work with parents to promote early literacy development. *Research Papers in Education*, 6 (2), 77-97.

Nutbrown, C., Hannon, P. and Weinberger, J. (in press) Training teachers to work with parents to promote early literacy development. *International Journal of Early Childhood*.

Weinberger, J., Hannon, P., & Nutbrown, C. (1990) *Ways of working with parents to promote early literacy development. USDE Papers in Education, No.14*. Sheffield. University of Sheffield Division of Education. [Available from Publication Sales, Division of Education, The University, Sheffield S10 2TN, England. Price £5.50 including overseas mail. Payment to 'University of Sheffield'.]

The accounts in this chapter are the result of an unusual collaboration between two researchers, one in France, the other in England. Their subjects are two children who are strangers to the culture and language of their schools, so they are struggling to make sense of what their teachers say to them and to understand the rituals of their classrooms. In their turn, the teachers stretch their undoubted skills to interpret the behaviour of their pupils, which they find puzzling. The detailed analyses of the interactions reveal the essential complexity of literacy, its social embeddedness, and the irrelevance of single definitions of its nature. As the teachers respond to the children, we see the need for subtle and sensitive pedagogies in situations such as these. The writers discover that, although their contexts are clearly different, they have common concerns. This example of one kind of comparison is a firm step on a new track of educational collaboration.

Chapter 2

TONY AND JEAN-FRANCOIS LOOKING FOR SENSE IN THE STRANGENESS OF SCHOOL

Evelyn Gregory and Jean Biarnès

Tony and Jean François set out to learn the secrets they know must be held in the books of their classrooms. Both come from cultures very distant from that of the school they enter, though both have teachers who are in different ways outstanding. Tony's teacher is sensitive to the cultural and linguistic differences of her children and visits their families with books for story-reading at home. Jean-François' teacher is active in a movement towards child-centred education in France. But both recognise that it is precisely the 'culture' of their pupils which is creating the problem.

The stories of these two children complement each other and at the same time reveal different sides of the same question. Jean-François shows us today what might become of Tony tomorrow. Both act as a mirror in which the words, 'If the culture of the teacher is to become part of the consciousness of the child, then the culture of the child must first be in the consciousness of the teacher' (Bernstein, 1973), may become a challenge for each teacher.

TONY

When 'Choosing' is so Hard:
Tony's entry into the British classroom

Tony begins school in a large multilingual reception class in Northampton, a town in the South Midlands. His parents and grandparents came to Britain from China via Hong Kong ten years ago. Tony is the only child from a Chinese background in his class, though there are enough children in the town for the parents to have organised a regular Saturday school where Tony learns to become literate in Mandarin. About 60% of Tony's classmates' families come from the Indian sub-continent and their children are learning English as a second or third language.

The teachers make a considerable effort to show that the school is part of the community it serves. There is a Community Centre providing English classes and a multilingual Lending Library, although, as yet, few parents use these facilities. Children are usually brought to school by grandfathers or older brothers, who leave them hurriedly at the school gate. The teachers feel distanced from the families through language and culture and concentrate their efforts on introducing the children to the British way of life. Stories and books play a special role in this introduction and the teachers try to send books home regularly with the children.

Tony enters school smiling, his eyes anxiously scanning the classroom which has been set out with activities for the children to choose from. During his first week, he quickly completes the 'Find your name' task and usually chooses to draw, making intricate copies of book covers with intense concentration.

He listens avidly at class discussions, his hand shooting up each time the teacher asks a question, though he is unable to reply when chosen. His teacher, Mrs G realises that Tony's parents have chosen to give him an English name and sees this as an indication of their aim to enable him to identify with the British culture in which he will probably live. His English Second Language teacher puts him in her 'advanced' group and praises him to the others: 'You know, don't you! You're good, you are!'

A month later, Tony's behaviour has undergone a complete change. His smile has disappeared, replaced in Mrs G's words, by a 'dead- pan look' which 'you can't seem to get through to'. Tony now spends most of his day in class wandering aimlessly around the room. He still draws, practising the same 'transformer' from all

Figure 5: 'A book cover copied by Tony at school when he was not quite five'

angles, but he throws his pictures away upon completion, refusing to take them home. He is a 'loner' and appears unable to play with other children. His class teacher says regretfully that he appears to have no interest whatsoever in school and has 'gone backwards'. His English Second Language teacher transfers him to her 'beginners' group', maintaining that she made a mistake in thinking that he knew more than he did. Mrs G is mystified by Tony's change in behaviour. He does not seem capable of choosing an activity or participating in sociodramatic play. She feels that his English is not improving because he is unable to 'jump in' and take risks safely, which play would allow him to do. She is also puzzled by his poor behaviour. Mrs G comments, 'It's unusual. The Vietnamese children usually do so well'.

'Processing' Words and 'Sharing' Stories

During his first week in school, Tony proudly brings a plastic bag and points out to the class during newstime that it has 'Chinese writing' on it. Mrs G thinks that Tony will enjoy reading and learn quickly. Her opinion seems justified when he constantly asks 'What's that?' over and over again as he points to an object in the illustration of a book she is reading with him. After several months, his continual questioning of detail has changed to become the regular repetition of the last word of the sentences he reads. By this time, she feels that Tony appears to have little interest in the stories upon which she bases her early reading tuition and that he wants to 'collect' or 'possess' words. At the end of his first year, he tries to avoid sharing books with her.

Below is an excerpt from one of his reading sessions after a year in school. She is reading a story with Tony which is most children's favourite: *Rosie's Walk* by Pat Hutchins (Penguin):

Mrs G: I like this story (points to a book) And I like that one, too (points)

Tony: I don't like that

Mrs G: Don't you?

Tony: It's a long story

Mrs G: Don't you like long stories?

Tony: No

20

Mrs G: No? Why not?

Tony: 'Cos I not. I want this one, not that one

Mrs G: OK (reads) 'Rosie's Walk'

Tony: What's that book? (points to another book)

Mrs G: That one's about dinosaurs. Let's leave that one for the moment, shall we?

The Talismanic Value of Books

A colleague of Mrs G's visits the parents as the children begin school. She is warmly invited into Tony's home and reports that his family are enthusiastic to help him in his 'homework'. When Tony does not want to take books home, Mrs G visits the family taking an attractive dual- language picture book which she hopes to leave them to read with Tony. She is surprised by the frosty reception she meets from his grandfather:

> 'Tony can't have this book yet. You must keep it and give it to him later.'
> 'But why?'
> 'Because he can't read the words. First he must learn to read the words, then he can have the book.'

Tony's grandfather pulls out an exercise-book from under the counter and shows it to the teacher. A number of pages have been filled with rows of immaculate ideographs. His grandfather says proudly that Tony has completed these at his Chinese Saturday school. With a sceptical look at the teacher, he pulls out a screwed-up piece of paper. On one side was a shop advertisement from which it had been recycled. On the other was a drawing of a transformer. Tony's grandfather:

> 'This is from his English school. This is rubbish.'

Pointing to the corner where 'ToNy' is written, he says,

> 'Look. He can't even write his name yet!'

Studies from psychology and anthropology tell us that the way children make sense of the world, the way past experiences are interpreted and future events predicted will be governed by their social and cultural background. This means that families who do not share the key concepts, sometime called 'core constructs' (Kelly,

1955) or 'primary message systems' (Hall 1959), represented by the teacher and school may have a different interpretation of what constitutes 'learning', 'school', 'play' 'teacher' etc. Ethnographic and classroom studies from the USA show how children bring different politeness and turn-taking routines as well as different ways of approaching literacy learning and stories into school.

It is true that Tony's family polarises key concepts which his teacher aims to reconcile in her teaching; 'play' opposes 'learning', 'teacher' opposes 'friend', 'hard work' opposes 'choice' For Tony's family, school represents practice and , 'hard work' into which the concepts of 'choice', 'play' or 'wanting to learn' do not enter. The teacher 'teaches' by providing information and then questioning the child; turntaking is made up of a 'question/answer' formula.

In Tony's family, books are valued highly and are given to a child as the just reward for learning to read. To provide a supply of books before this, devalues both the book itself and the concept of hard work. Likewise, each written ideograph must be practised until it is perfect; one stroke out of place changes its whole meaning. Attention to detail and examining the look of a symbol is particularly important, since a number of ideographs are pictorial. Tony's version of his name and other words he experiments with writing in his English classroom, would simply be wrong in Mandarin script.

Buttressing the views of Tony's family is a long respect for literacy where, over centuries, the 'literati' or highly literate held immense power in society. This tradition of respect is reflected today in the existence of a special 'educated' or 'beautiful' script alongside the ordinary script. Mastery of the 'beautiful' script needs years of concentration and hard work. It is so special that children relate it to a folk tale 'The Chicken with Golden Eggs' (The Golden Goose). Attempting to rush the learning of this script will only spoil it. It is so complex that Chinese students spend the first year of their Language and Literature degree learning to perfect it.

The Danger of 'Models' of Learning and Early Childhood Education

Mrs G has very different ideas on how school learning takes place and her role as teacher within it. Mrs G follows a child-centred approach in her teaching, believing that early school learning is best promoted through giving children the freedom to take risks and to experiment, and through the provision of ample materials. Her classroom is well-equipped for this, with a number of imaginative activities which the sociodramatic play area and children can choose from during most of the day. Most children respond well to the relaxed atmosphere she has created.

A similar approach is taken in her teaching of early literacy. She believes that children learn to read and write by experimenting and taking risks, by 'having a go'. Tony's teacher sees herself as providing children with a model of a skilled practitioner, whereby the children learn beside her as apprentices, gradually sharing and partnering her in the reading. Mrs G is also familiar with research studies showing how a knowledge of written stories enables a child to step quickly into reading and she aims to provide children with interesting stories which they will want to take home and share with their parents.

The difficulties of children like Tony are often explained in terms of his cultural background, which is very different from that of his teacher and the institution she represents. The poor progress of children from minority-group backgrounds is seen to stem from a discontinuity in discourse and learning systems from home to school. We tend to assume that our views based on current educational theory are right and that it is the child rather than the teacher who must adapt . After her colleague's home visits, Mrs G says that she realises that Tony's family would prefer to see more formal teaching methods used in school. She feels she cannot comply with their wishes on the grounds that they contradict her 'child-centred' approach to learning.

That Mrs. G. sees no contradiction in equating her own approach to teaching with being 'child-centred' highlights clearly the difficulties we all face as teachers. On the one hand, we aim to start from where each individual child stands, treating children as unique individuals with very different learning experiences. On the other, we feel the pressure to work within currently promoted theories of learning in order to show ourselves as 'good' teachers who are well-read in current theories of teaching and learning. But can we really be sure that children who are familiar with stories from home inherently learn to read more easily or might it have more to do with the approach and materials their teachers use? Do children necessarily need play activities successfully to master formal school learning? Are informal relationships between teacher and learner automatically more conducive to a child's learning? There is a danger that we come to regard currently accepted theories as unassailable 'models' rather than culturally specific beliefs.

The pressure upon us as teachers to show ourselves as knowledgeable of current ideas and to teach children to read within their framework means that we are in danger of accepting deficit myths to explain children's lack of progress. Children's difficulties may be explained through a lack of stories from home, illiterate parents or their different ideas of school, literacy and learning. In a way, Tony is a victim of one form of this. His teachers expect him 'as a Vietnamese child' to work within their interpretation of learning because 'they always do well'. The irony behind the myth here is the mistaken nationality. In contrast with Vietnamese families, who tend to aim primarily at British values, families from Hong Kong try hard to preserve traditional values.

Focus on a discontinuity of learning systems between child and school does not help Tony and his teacher because this means that we assume that children will expect to find similar 'ways of learning' in home and school and cannot cope with difference. To some extent, all children starting school expect to meet a 'new world' in terms of new demands on language and behaviour. Indeed, children from very different cultural and linguistic backgrounds have been shown to be more able to see through to the linguistic and cultural demands of a totally new world by seeing school through the eyes of a 'stranger'.

It is more helpful to begin by examining the strengths both bring into school. Tony, his family and his teacher were all enthusiastic when he started school. We see how each 'worked hard' within their own expectations of what was needed to succeed. But these expectations remained implicit and unvoiced. The demands made by Tony's Chinese school are made explicit and clear and it would make sense to expect the same from his English school. When this does not happen, Tony appears to 'switch off'. Tony's family see only the result on paper of his English learning. They do not have the opportunity to discuss explicitly why his teacher works in this way. Tony's teacher implicitly expects Tony and his parents to understand and share her view of learning without their actually understanding what it might be. Rather than a discontinuity of learning systems, the essence of Tony's difficulties might well be that no discontinuity is expected.

JEAN-FRANÇOIS

When the Teacher Thinks she Knows:
Jean François in Paris

It is a November morning in a School in an eastern suburb of Paris. The class has 30 year five children — nine and ten year olds. The area is very mixed socially, consisting of middle managers, factory workers and shop keepers. At least 15% of the children have one parent or more who is unemployed. A little more than 29% of the school population are of immigrant origin, the majority from North Africa or Portugal. This percentage does not include children whose parents are from France's overseas territories, like Jean François.

He came from Guadeloupe four years ago and is now ten. His mother lives on her own with her three sons. Jean François is the eldest and the only child to have been born back home. From his great age of ten, he feels responsible for looking after his younger brothers who go to the Nursery. His mother gives her children every possible affection, but she spends long hours as a nurse, working in a suburb a long way from her home.

Continuing the Story

When Jean François comes into the classroom with his friends, the teacher has already written a text of five lines on the blackboard with the date and the title 'Logic' above. Underneath/ separated by a space, there are the beginnings of two sentences. The text refers to a short story, in which it is difficult to work out who is who and who does what. The children have to complete the two sentences to show that they have understood the logic of the situation. The teacher explains this to the children by saying:

> 'Today, it's not me who is telling you the story. It's written on the board, and if you don't read it carefully, you won't be able to continue it. Work in silence for five minutes and I'll see what you come up with.'

When she asks for answers five minutes later, ten hands go up, including Jean François'. She asks him to read out his work. Jean François has, indeed, used the beginnings of the two sentences, but has continued by imagining his own endings. The teacher says:

25

'That's typical of you Jean-François, you've got your head in the clouds. You're always dreaming, *mon grand*, but that's not what I asked for.'

When I spoke to him later, he said that the teacher had been 'unfair' because she had told them 'to continue the story' and, in any case, 'she never says I've done anything right'.

Jean François seems to have been unable to interpret the teacher's meaning when she used the words 'continue the story'. For the other children, 'continue the story' is the 'code' which calls up the words 'today it's not me who is going to tell you the story'. These words enable most children to switch into a specific familiar classroom exercise, the only difference being the presence of the written text for reference on the board. The children needed to draw upon their knowledge of past classroom exercises to know what was expected of them.

'If you don't read carefully, you won't be able to continue the story' is interpreted by Jean François as simply, 'read carefully and continue the story'.

Most children completed the task without difficulty, so how can we understand why Jean François, and perhaps some others like him, were unable to do likewise?

Given the time of day, we can hardly blame this on a lack of attention, although this is the teacher's explanation. Instead, we might draw on another example of discourse for some help in understanding Jean François' difficulty. Here two mothers are speaking to their children about the same situation at the school gate:

> 1st Mother: 'Xavier, your shoe-lace is undone and you'll fall over if you step on it'
>
> 2nd Mother: 'Albert, your shoe-lace!'
>
> Xavier and Albert both do their laces up, whilst saying to themselves:
>
> Xavier: 'If I step on my lace, I'll fall over and smash my face in'.
>
> Albert: 'My shoe-lace again!'

This example shows how differently tasks can be coded linguistically.

If we return to Jean François, we find similarities between the teacher and Xavier's mother in how they formulate a task. This is not surprising as both represent the same 'mainstream' background, but for children like Jean François, it is often the beginning of a history of school failure.

But how does the teacher react after Jean François' mistake?

'That's typical of you' simply reinforces a history of failure. 'You've always got your head in the clouds, you're dreaming' is simply another way of telling Jean François that he is never able to understand anything and it accounts for his complaint, 'She never says I've done anything right'.

Finally, although the teacher uses the term *'mon grand'* apparently with affection, she is in fact doing something rather different. Jean François is one year older than his class mates as he has had to repeat a class. Her words, therefore, serve only to draw further attention to his failure.

The teacher's subconsciously negative approach constantly reinforces Jean François' failure and may well prevent him from learning in class. When Jean François says, 'It's not fair', he is openly announcing that he has resigned himself to the situation. The aggression of five-year old Tony has been replaced in a ten-year old by resignation .

'Kabann-la'

Several months later, we meet Jean François in a 'vocabulary' lesson. A large picture has been pinned to the board, showing a market garden with the gardener, the vegetables, the garden tools and a shed to keep them in. Jean François is being questioned. He replies to the first questions correctly. But the teacher then asks him:

'Is it like that in your country ?'

'No miss' says Jean François and starts describing his grandfather's garden. His teacher interrupts him abruptly, saying

'Good. Now show me the shed.'

Jean François looks at the picture and stays silent. The teacher insists:

'Come on, show me the shed.'

Jean François looks away from the picture to the teacher, his face questioning, his body frozen.

The teacher sends him back to his seat, saying 'Well, Jean François, are you tired? Go back to your place. Who can show me the shed?.'

The sudden change in the child's posture is not enough to make the teacher question her reaction. Her response 'Are you tired?' springs directly from stereotypes of immigrants from the tropics. If Jean François had been from any other foreign country, the teacher would have asked herself whether the child had understood the word 'cabanne' (shed). And if she had asked Jean François, he would have answered:

'Yes, miss, it's for sleeping on. It has four legs and a mattress.'

The word 'kabann-la' means 'bed' in Creole. The question was posed in the context of Jean François grandfather's garden and he interprets the words within this 'cultural space'. There is no bed in the picture he is describing and, in addition, the teacher asks her question using the Creole grammar 'Show me the 'cabanne' (shed/bed) there!'

When we spoke to him, Jean François said 'I wondered what the teacher was talking about!'

Conclusion

The examples given in this chapter illustrate clearly the meaning of our opening quotation, that the culture of the child must become part of the culture of the teacher. The complexity presented by these two cases shows the naivete of the 'solution' that the teacher must 'know' the culture of the child. One cannot 'know' a culture from the outside: a culture cannot explicitly be 'taught'. Attempting to adopt a child's culture may be even more dangerous than doing nothing at all, for the cultural 'traits' learned by the teacher may well lead to creating new stereotypes which she believes to be more 'realistic' but which do nothing to further her understanding.

But what should the teacher do to help? Should she for example change her own way of speaking to that of different children? Even a moment's reflection shows how impossible this would be. However, the teacher can become aware of her own cultural interpretations and her own ways of speech. Only by having this awareness can she make explicit to the children the exact linguistic requirements of each particular situation in which they find themselves. In this case, if the teacher had known that she was using a linguistic code which was unfamiliar to some of the children in her class, it would have sufficed to say, 'Listen, I'm going to give you a task.' Not only would Jean François and others like him have understood the whole interaction as being a task but those children who are tied within the coding of 'your shoe-lace' would have learned that school tasks are likely to be encoded in a specific way.

Finally being aware of 'how I speak' enables a child to realise that different registers can be used for different situations. By enabling children to 'play' with different registers, the teacher is showing them the arbitrariness of different words to represent objects, thereby giving children access to the basic tools of mastering their language.

The stories of Tony and Jean François show the importance of 'asking the right questions' as a precondition to creating a classroom 'culture'. This culture must be actively negotiated by all the class and must allow space for different understandings and conflicts. The role of the teacher within this culture will be as a 'mediator' who facilitates a child's entry into a new world, an entry vital for future school success.

Bibliography

Bernstein, B. (1973) *Class, Codes and Control*. Vol. II. Herts. Paladin. p. 225.

Bruner, B. (1986) *Actual Minds, Possible Worlds*. Cambridge, Mass.:Harvard University Press.

Heath, S.B. (1983) *Ways with Words: Language, Life and Work in Communities and Classrooms*. Cambridge: CUP.

Vygotsky, L. (1978) *Mind in Society: The development of higher psychological processes*. Cambridge, Mass: Harvard University Press.

The classical studies of individual children learning to write show how insightful adults follow the inclinations of the learners to make meanings that can be shared with others. Success seems to come when an adult responds to what children want to write by guiding their attempts to master the distinctive features of the writing system. Here we see Elena making a book and at the same time showing her teacher how she can help her. Esperanza Miguel Gutierrez emphasises the social nature of classroom writing and the importance of collaborating with parents who will then understand how writing is taught in school.

The writing activity also lets the researcher investigate the *deep play* of children's storytelling. In a postscript, J. Kino Barrio Valencia explains how this kind of teacher action research, with its emphasis on the writer's intention to make meaningful narratives, helps to 'close the gap between the findings of academic research on writing and educational reality'. Meanwhile, Elena, the heroine of the piece, makes gallant strides.

Chapter 3

MUM THREW MY STORY
INTO THE BIN

Esparanza Pilar Gutiérrez
with postscript by J Lino Barrio Valencia

Introduction

When I became involved in the writing research project at the
University of Valladolid, I was working with children of four in a
school in the centre of Valladolid. The building dates from the time
of the Republic. Although it has been modernised inside, it still
retains the features of schools constructed in that period. It has big
windows and is very spacious, although the courtyards are small.
In general, the children are from the middle classes (professionals,
civil servants, business people, etc.). The school follows the policy
of integrating children with motor deficiencies, so in every class
there are two children with special needs. That year in my class
there happened to be a hemiplegic boy and a girl with progressive
urticaria.

With these four-year-olds I was trying to encourage the development of a set of behaviour patterns and habits which would be
appropriate for the level of maturity natural to this age group, the
main activities being oral expression and understanding, the hand-

ling and exploring of different materials, motor co-ordination, bodily expression, painting and modelling. We did a lot of drama activities, told lots of stories, recited poems and sang.

When the research project was introduced in the centre, I thought it would be interesting to work in a team with colleagues, sharing points of view, checking theories, all with a view to gaining a more thorough evaluation of my work in the classroom, as well as of the children's progress. Even though my children were four-year-olds, the writing theme attracted my attention. I had noticed that they frequently scribbled on their drawings and imitated my writing.

The first thing I realised was that these graphic activities were not only a sign of pictorial-motor development, but that the children were experimenting with written language. At that point my outlook changed. I adopted the initial focus of the research, to get a more accurate idea of what the children really knew. This led me to collect data on the children's first steps in writing and the ways in which they talked about it. I thus acquired a solid base from which to supply them with the help they needed.

This is a brief synopsis of how I started to work on the project. I mention those beginnings now, because I saw that the type of work they were suggesting we should do could be very useful to me in my classroom practice and its effects on the children. The effort of collating data, the renewed interest in attending individually to each child, the careful attention to their points of view, the discussion with colleagues outside the classroom and the constant reappraisal of what I was doing, were all factors which encouraged me to carry on.

Out of all the data, activities and experiments with which we have been involved during these last few years, I want to concentrate on one of the activities which proved to be most interesting and fruitful in the development of writing: making up stories.

The Story Corner

In the following year, with the same children, now five, there came a moment when I set myself the following problem: how to plan free activities so that they would also be useful to the most advanced children.

In general my class was organised in the following way: as soon as the children came in, they greeted each other, talked about their day-to-day concerns, changed, showed what they had brought in, then they spontaneously chose the kind of activity they wanted to do. For this I had prepared several areas with lots of different materials: construction materials, plastic activities, weighing, measuring volume, reading, graphic activities, logical and mathematical activities. After these activities we all came together so they could tell everybody what they had done, what they had learned, what they had discovered, sharing their findings with each other. Finally, we carried out activities with the whole group.

I had frequently observed that when they first started the free activities, some children devoted themselves to writing in their own way, obviously. For example, they tried to write and draw stories they invented. By then the children already knew quite a few letters, and in their spontaneous writing most of them came into the so-called syllabic category, or into the transition to the alphabetical category (Ferreiro and Terberosky, 1979).

There were others, however, who never chose that kind of activity. Although afterwards, during the structured activity period, they all worked together on different aspects of writing, it was evident that the group that engaged in these 'writing' activities was making faster progress than the others.

The problem I had set myself, as I've already said, was to give the more advanced group the opportunity to continue making good progress. What I was looking for was a way to create a situation in which the free writing activities could motivate both groups. I wanted to foster an interest in writing in the second group, while enabling the first to move on. Based on my observation of the kind of activities enjoyed by the first group, and the way they periodically exchanged ideas with their classmates, I organised what I called the story corner.

The children were accustomed to using the stories we had in class. I often read stories aloud and made use of the occasion to show the children where the title was, the author's name, the page numbers. It seemed a good idea to encourage them not only to write stories but to write books like the ones they so enjoyed handling. It was not difficult to imagine the form the books would take: the covers could be made with cardboard; inside would go the pages, suitably numbered and stapled together. Naturally, we would have the title, the author's name and even that of the publisher. The text and illustrations would be theirs. They could work individually or in groups. They could start with the illustrations or the text. They could use the computer or write by hand. Whichever way they did it, the final product would be a book.

Figure 6: 'Spontaneous story writing'

Elena

A book is something very serious. It's something other people can read — Miss, classmates and also mums and dads. It can't be written any old way. Elena knew that very well, because when she read out the story she had written in December, 'The Little Flying Birds', something odd happened. Elena could 'read' perfectly. But when her friend tried to read it, she read:

The little birds that fly.' And then:

'e-p-a-i-t-o-d-e-t l-o-r-a-s-u-m-a...'

Until, clearly tired by the effort of identifying the words letter by letter, she stopped and said: 'But I can't understand any of it!'

Others tried, with the same result. Elena picked up her story again:

'The thing is, there are a few letters missing.' And she looked very thoughtful

This is the transcription of Elena's story. I've used the double stroke // to indicate a change of page. It is only an approximate transcription!

Elena's writing	English translation
epaito — det	*lil berz
lorasumama	thermumskring
ioaiesaufiz//	ane
etoz — seaoaotap — zaoes	then —
rrio — ueouaoru	larft — went
p//	
ietoz — esue — oauo	anthen — hewent —
ito — zfeofi — z	lil —
po — oeiauc amigo //	pore — frend //
iet — z — ieto — zes	
asenoa — roias	
uie — rsesudeo	flize — it hapnd
iseose	an it hapnd lik that

In the previous year I had already realised how enormously important it is to encourage a child to try to write. As and when a few letters and a few words gradually started to appear, my response was always positive: 'fantastic'. But the step towards conventional alphabetical writing is a very hard one. It isn't good enough any more just to copy what the adult words or text look like, or to interpret them syllabically. The child must become more accurate at identifying the phonemes and rendering the conventional graphic symbols which correspond to them. The enormous effort involved in these tasks is only justified if the child has a huge desire to write. In this case, to write her own books.

Elena went on writing. One morning in January she was reading a story from the library. It was called 'The Little School'. Then she started to write. She had the story in front of her. She copied some sentences, and invented others. She gave it a new title: 'The Mayor who Built a School'. In the text appear sentences taken from the book, together with some she had made up. If we compare it with what we saw before, there are notable differences:

THE MAYOR WHO BUILT A SCHOOL//

THE MAYOR WHO BUI //

the house which the children come. // the cuntry is sad // the cuntry is hapy, now // neanw le the others were playing run ing games // Peso — camo they all sangat the sam time letsgo fishing // but the mayor. the ma yor woz bilding a school // thanks — very much for — making us a school END // /

Days later I saw her writing on a piece of paper.

'What are you doing, Elena?'

'I'm playing at making up words.'

Some of the words she has written were up on wall cards. Others were not. She was copying, but she was learning. I remembered the babbling of young children when they are playing at saying things or simply making sounds. They are playing and learning. In much the same way, Elena was exploring her own writing.

A colleague who was working on the writing project with older children had asked her pupils to write a story to send to the other classes in the school. They made up a pre-school version and one morning they told it to us. The story was called 'The three clouds'. Afterwards, we did a number of activities around it. And finally, a number of stories were written, stories which differed from the original. But before making the book the children had to be very careful to write properly in a way that could be read by others.

Figure 7: 'From Elenás story, The Mayor who Built a School'

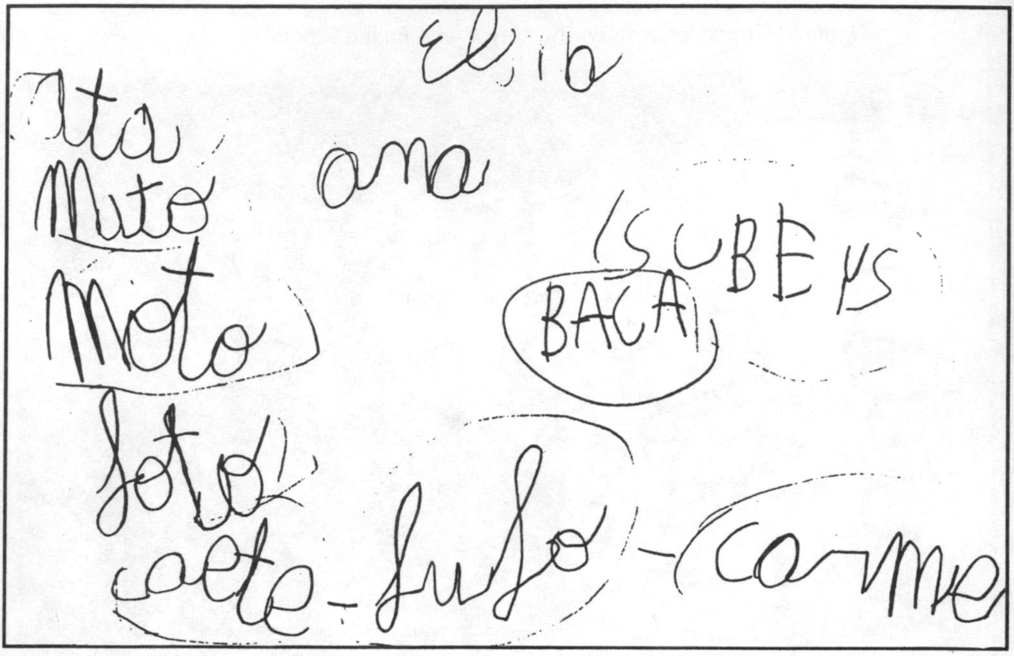

Figure 8: 'Elena's made-up words'

Elena had made a first attempt at her cloud story (1). That morning the class included two students on teacher training practice and Lino, from the University research team, had come to pay us a visit. One of the students began to work with Elena on her story, while Lino made notes. Isabel, the student, read out Elena's first text, phonetically analysing each word, pronouncing each phoneme carefully so that Elena would recognise it and write the appropriate graphic symbol. As a result, the story changed in both graphics and meaning (2):

(1)

The four clouds
wanted
to make a storm
but one got lost

could not
make a storm
but
(remainder indistinct)

40

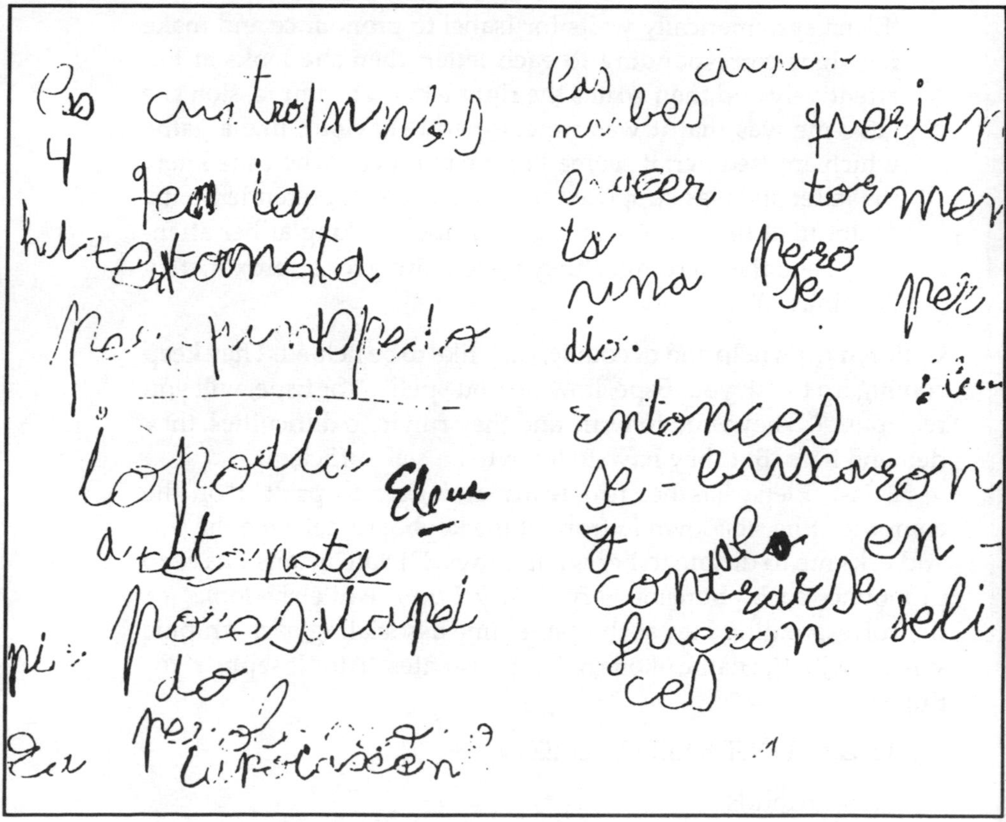

Figure 9: 'Elena's first and second versions of The Four Clouds'

(2)
The four
clouds wanted
to make a storm
but
one got lost
then they looked
for one another
and on
finding each other
they were happy.

Lino passed me the following annotations:

'Elena systematically waits for Isabel to pronounce and make the signs corresponding to each letter; then she looks at her attentively and then writes the right letter. The impression she gave me was that it was stereotyped behaviour, like a game which amused her; it seemed to me that even when she knew the letter she was supposed to write, she still pretended to be doubtful at first, kept waiting for Isabel, looking at her attentively, and then writing... (they were writing for approximately 25 minutes)'.

Children need help and of course, they like to be helped. They keep coming up to ask you 'Espe, how do you spell...?' or Espe, will you read out...?' They want to write and they run in to difficulties. they demand help. But they have to learn to be self-sufficient.

At last, Elena has her text ready and goes to print it on the computer. She sits down in front of the keyboard, tells me the text and asks me to dictate to her what it says. Dictate means I have to pronounce each phoneme very clearly. I do it while she looks for the corresponding key, at the same time associating each graphic symbol with the name of one of her classmates: 'j' for Joseph, 'r' for Ruben...

THE 4 CLOUDS ELENA DIEZ/ /

the 4 urclouds/ /

The four clouds wanted to make a storm but one of them got lost. Then they looked for each other and when they met up they were happy. Elena / /

THE 4 CLOUDS ELENA ROBLES DIEZ END / /

Published 2nd year pre-school

They also wrote about clouds in groups. But by then they must have been tired, because only Elena wanted to finish it:

TOR MEN TA SI   YES ST OR M

Elena Robles Diez second year of pre-school / /

Once upon a time there were 4 clouds who did want to make a storm
(*tormenta*) with thunder and lightening. *tor ta men ta* / /
we want to make a storm and Men said we'll go to a cuntry and Tor said: then

Figure 10: 'The Dolphin in the water'

el delfin
en el agua

Elena Robles, 2ª de preescolar

children won't bo ther us *tor men ta* / /
they got to the cuntry which started to rai n and then they felt
at ease *tor men*
ta/ /
and as they threw them out of that cuntry, they left that cuntry.
— *tor men ta* / /
here are our friends in this cuntry, *tor men ta* / / here they stayed
in this other
cuntry. -/ /
THE END

It is curious to observe how one fine day the story was supposed
to be finished: 'Then the children won't bother us'. But the next day
she carried on writing it on her own, adding a new ending: 'And
as they threw them out of that cuntry, they left that cuntry'. After a
time, she felt the need to do some more work on the story and added
the final little touch: 'Here are our friends in this cuntry. Here they
stayed in this other cuntry'.

I mentioned the computer earlier. Although it is not central to
my story, I would like to comment on one of the functions it
fulfilled. I had the chance to get access to a computer and printer
in my classroom, thanks to my participation in the Atenea Project
and in the programme for the integration of handicapped children.
The primary objective was to help all the children with special
needs. But soon it was used by all the children. As far as writing is
concerned, it was efficient in helping to eliminate obstacles to the
customary first steps leading to conventional writing. It was the
same thinking which led me to use the little printing press and
scratched letters: to prevent grapho-motor difficulties impeding
children expressing themselves in writing. Amongst the software
available was an art package. So the computer became a stimulus
to writing. It supplied us with characters about which the children
subsequently wrote stories.

That was what happened with the book which Elena made in
class. On the title page we can see the dolphin obtained from the
graphic program, the title and the author's name:

the dolphin
in the water

Elena Robles, 2nd year of pre-school

Elena and Vicki

The importance of collaboration between school and family, especially in the early years of schooling, can never be over stressed. Perhaps the ideal thing would be to establish a continuity between the two environments, so that the children don't feel a brusque rupture when they cross the barriers separating the two. Certainly during the school year when the work discussed here was undertaken, the situation was very close to that ideal. The atmosphere of collaboration created was very positive. Periodically we had meetings which were attended by fathers and mothers. I explained the steps the children were taking down the road towards writing, showing them the work they were doing in class. I was convinced about what I was doing so was able to convince them about my way of working. I always stressed the need for collaboration: for talking to the children, telling them stories, attending to their demands, reading and writing with them, attaching positive value to their achievements and stimulating their desire to learn. The parents usually reacted with curiosity and amazement at something they had not experienced. At the meeting they themselves brought up the conversations they were having with their children. The questions ᵢhey were being asked at home, the help for which they were being asked: How shall I put...?' The questions were no different from the things that I was being asked in class.

I realise that the degree of collaboration with the parents is related to their socio-cultural conditions — as research has shown. But my experience at present is more eloquent. I am currently working in a rural school, also with pre-school children aged five. A moment ago I was talking about continuity, yet now I am experiencing the consequences of a breakdown in relations between family and school, and trying with difficulty to build a bridge which will bring them together.

In the case of Elena, the collaboration could not have been more satisfactory. As well as what she in wrote in class, she often brought me things she had written at home: stories, letters, poems, news items, etc. In class one morning, she handed me a book she had made at home. On the title-page, she had dedicated the book to her dad. Inside, each page contained a drawing of a fruit accompanied by an explanatory text. I took some time to realise that the most important thing was on the opposite page. That was where she usually put her name, the name of the author. In the one that she handed to me there was written:

45

Figure 11: 'Joint authors'

I came across an example of the opposite a few days ago in my new school, Alicia arrived in class crying. She had spent several days writing her first book. At last she finished it. She wanted to take it home, so I put it in a folder for her so that it wouldn't get marked. I told her to read it to dad and mum.

'What's the matter, Alicia?'

'My mum threw my story in the bin.'

After talking to her mother, I managed to get the story back. I shall keep it always. The binding is stained with tomato sauce.

Writing More and More

That year Elena wrote many stories. She undoubtedly learned how to write. In the study of the products of writing, many interesting phenomena may be observed: one can see the signs of a difficult, non-linear process, going backwards and forwards, sometimes faltering, with momentary successes being set back by difficulties which had apparently already been overcome. In short, there is no constant progression. Overall one can see how children's ability to tell stories is increasing, how they are breaking away from the immediate context, how the relationship between illustration and text is changing. And also, of course, how the graphic quality of their writing is improving.

On the other hand, story-writing and book-making is only one aspect of the work developed, and only part of the texts Elena wrote. She also wrote letters to her parents and to me she wrote news items, footnotes to photos, advertisements, comics, inscriptions... I guided her into many such kinds of writing. But on many occasions it was she who asked to write, and asked if she could do it in a different way. To that end she would look for graphics programs on the computer which would provide her with new topics, she looked for new formats for the books, she even sought out new difficulties.

One of the last pieces of work she did in class in the way of stories is the one called 'The Vase'. She told me she wanted to do a very, very small story. She looked in the computer graphics for a pot and some flowers, but couldn't find anything. In the end she decided to print out a flower vase, the nearest image to the one she wanted that she could find. With this as a reference point, she wrote her story in less than ten minutes:

The Vase

There was once a pot who hadn't got any water and as it couldn't//
walk or move, as the water was near, it got hold of it by itself//
and was happy to drink and drink and jackanory//
this is the end of the story. The end
(*colorin colarado este cuento se ha acabado. Fin.*)

Conclusion

Remembering Elena's case now, I attach even more importance to the collaboration between parents and the pre-school centre. The problem I have to set myself now is to foster the learning of writing in an illiterate society. As well as my work in the classroom I have inevitably to think about working with the parents, so they can appreciate their children's efforts, back them up in their learning, and understand the way we are trying to support them at school. As to written language, I feel strongly that any literacy programme for the children must be paralleled by a literacy programme aimed at the parents. The target might be that I manage to get a child coming into school showing me a story signed by him and his mother. Meanwhile, I shall carry on wiping the tomato stains off their book bindings.

Postscript

by J Lino Barrio Valencia

This work by Esperanza Miguel is part of her collaboration in the University of Valladolid project, 'Study of children's writing in a school context by means of action-research', Research project approved within the General Promotion of Knowledge Programme (PB87-0089). For the project as a whole we set ourselves the following targets:

To increase our knowledge of children's writing in a school context, by

- analysing the problems confronted by children when they first start learning to write;
- analysing the problems confronted by children when they aspire to self-expression and communication in writing;
- studying what writing is used for at school;

48

- developing strategies which will help to increase children's ability to use writing for different purposes, so that it will contribute to their development as people capable of self-expression and communication.

We are also aiming:

- to make an immediate contribution to the professional development of the teacher engaged in the research and to the improvement of the quality of teaching, through research based on reflection, analysis and discussion of classroom problems, putting the suggested solutions into practice and checking the results;
- to establish practical forms of collaboration and mutual enrichment between preliminary and ongoing teacher training.

The principal intention of the research team was therefore to analyse the problems of children faced with the task of writing in school, and to study the means by which teachers can help them.

What follows is a brief outline of some of the basic aspects of the project.

1. Perspective on writing

Through experience of working with teachers at compulsory education levels, we knew that evaluating or even just talking about the pupils' writing, the graphic or transcriptional aspects such as spelling, handwriting and punctuation nearly always came up first. Only afterwards were other aspects mentioned such as expression and composition. This classroom situation has its parallel in the academic world. In our country, it is only in the last few years that writing has begun to be studied from a broader perspective, starting from the contributions of psycholinguistics, cognitive psychology and especially textual linguistics, together with work more closely linked to school practice.

With this in mind, and without denying the importance of the graphic aspects of writing — which would be to deny the evidence — we wanted to focus the research project on what is 'not graphic' in writing.

1. Children's writing in a school context

Of all the different ways of tackling research into writing, we opted for the study of children's writing in school. School is the institution where it is expected that children will formally and systematically perform a series of learning tasks, one of which is writing. From the schooling point of view, it is possible to talk of a moment when the child first starts learning to write, and of a period of years over which the learning skill is developed. It was not our aim to focus preferentially on any one of these moments, although the work presented here is limited to children aged four to five years in the pre-school period.

Our interest, then, lay in concentrating on the study of what was happening in the classroom in relation to writing. We kept away from other ways of studying children's writing, for we thought that our perspective would be more useful viewed from an educational standpoint. For example, it did not seem appropriate to design an experimental research project, so we were not interested in controlling any variables; on the contrary, we wanted to try to capture the way in which all of them influenced children's writing.

2. By means of action-research

From the academic perspective gained as university lecturers, we were conscious of the very large gap between the findings of academic research on writing and educational reality. We were also conscious of the difficulty of bridging the gap between both worlds.

Through contacts established with CARE (The Centre for Action Research in Education at the University of East Anglia, UK) we knew of different projects which had been carried out following the line of action-research based largely on the work of L. Stenhouse and J. Elliot. A research model rooted in classroom performance and aiming to further our knowledge as well as promote curricular and staff development seemed to us supremely apt as a methodological framework for our project.

In action research teachers monitor their own performance. If this principle is taken seriously, certain important consequences derive from it about the roles in a research project. This meant that the role of the university research group was to facilitate the research task of the teachers in the classroom, and to analyse their methodological problems — secondary research. The teachers working on the project were the ones doing research in their own work.

This, then, is the framework in which to place the work of Esperanza Miguel, pre-school teacher. In it she presents one aspect of her research. She has consciously avoided erudite language in order to make her work more accessible. She therefore adopts a direct narrative style which shows us, by means of a concrete example — the case of Elena — the type of problems arising when young children are encouraged to learn to write, and ways in which she tried to solve them. She uses the child's writing to show the development which took place during the course of the year.

The value which this kind of narrative may have does not lie in its general applicability, as is the case with the demands of experimental research. Indeed, no such kind of general applicability is the aim here. But readers — and especially if they are questioning their own activities in the classroom — can compare their own experiences and situations with what is described in the text. In the final analysis it is readers who can decide to what extent the example is applicable to their own cases.

References

Cohen, R. (1977) *L'Apprentissage Prècoce de la Lecture* Paris: PUF

Ferreiro, E. (1979) *Los Sistemas de Escritura en el Desarrollo del Nino* Mexico: Siglo XXI

Medrano, G. (1975) 'Preparacion de un ambiente enriquecido en el aula de preescolar'
1. Jornadas Nacionales de Educacion Preescolar Malaga pp.17-21

Stenhouse, L. (1975) *An Introduction to Curriculum Research and Development* London: Heinemann

Tonucci, F. (1976) *A Tre Anni si Fa Ricerca* Firenze: Lib. Ed. Florentina

Collaboration between teachers and parents is now seen as necessary and important — inevitable, even. But decades of separation of the roles of home and school in the upbringing and education of children have often resulted in misunderstandings between those who have their development at heart. These differences are most acute when the social class and educational experience of the parents are different from those of the teachers. Early experiments in collaboration were often regarded with suspicion by parents who resented what they thought was interference. Teachers saw their overtures to parents treated with disdain. In Chapter 1 we saw how the researchers concentrated on the details of family life as the beginning of literacy. Now we see teachers learning to reinterpret the meaning of 'parental involvement.'

Tower Hamlets is the name of a community in East London. Historically its populations have been the immigrant poor. The University of Greenwich is a large institution of higher education where those who are responsible for the formation and education of school teachers are regularly required to work in schools. This chapter is about the vital planning which must precede the establishing of four-fold partnership of children, parents, teachers and researchers.

Chapter 4

GETTING STARTED ON THE PICC PROJECT

Roger Hancock, Penny Smith, Geoff Sheath,
Florence Bettlestone

The Reason for a Home School Project

Tower Hamlets is an inner-city, multicultural area in east London characterised by high unemployment and poverty. The area has a fast-growing population, — the result of a very high birth rate and an in-flow of people to the developing dockland areas.

These factors produce real challenges for education. There are difficulties both in finding school places for children and in the recruitment of teachers. Recently, in order to relieve teacher shortage, the Education Authority brought in teachers from America, Bangladesh, Holland and Southern Ireland.

Teaching in Tower Hamlets is particularly demanding of the skill and understanding of teachers. For many of the children, English is not their first language and many are not experienced in formal schooling. In addition, some suffer daily from racial harassment, particularly those from the Bangladeshi community. A number of children are transported to and from school daily by taxi to protect them from such harassment.

A constructive way of tackling some of these difficulties is to help parents participate in the school curriculum and the educational process. This holds out the possibility of all parties — parent, teacher and child — learning together. And it enables teachers to forge links with the rich cultural and linguistic traditions of the area.

The Structure of the Project

In 1989, most Tower Hamlets schools were involving parents in children's reading. However, many said they experienced difficulties in linking with parents because of demands made on teacher energy and time, and the difficulties associated with parents who were not confident in spoken and written English.

Following discussions between the University of Greenwich and Tower Hamlets Education Authority, it was decided to set up a project to help three schools develop their links with parents.

The project is based in a nursery and two primary schools. One member of our team (Roger Hancock) is coordinating and evaluating the project. The others (Penny Smith, Geoff Sheath and Florence Bettlestone) spend some time each week working in classrooms to promote parental involvement in children's language and literacy, in maths and in science. Together, lecturers and teachers are developing ways of sharing educational ideas with parents and listening to their views about children's learning.

Money to support the project has come from the University of Greenwich , Tower Hamlets and the London Docklands Development Corporation. The project is therefore a creative partnership between the university and the three schools, designed to give support to a key educational idea. The schools benefit from more resources and more teachers, and we welcome an opportunity to renew our school-based experience. In addition, there is the hope that everyone will be stimulated by being involved in exciting research.

Development in the three schools

The reports that follow have been compiled from our project notes and diaries and are based on seven half-day visits to the schools. We have tried to write in a direct and honest way about this very early but important phase in the project's life. We reveal our difficulties, our hopes and our plans. We also share what we mean by parental involvement in children's education and how we want to translate this understanding into school practice. With regard to the process of translation, it is apparent that we have set about this in slightly different ways with our own particular style and set of priorities. This personal freedom is important as it allows us to utilise our individual strengths and to take full account of the differences between schools.

School One: a Nursery School (for children aged 3-4)

The school is located in an area where the old Victorian terraced housing has been mainly replaced by unprepossessing blocks of flats. The school receives children from a wide variety of cultural backgrounds — English, Bangladeshi, African, Scottish, Caribbean, Irish, Chinese, Turkish. The largest ethnic groups are English and Bangladeshi. The school itself is set in grounds which are very unusual for an inner-city location. There is very generous and pleasing play space with grass, garden plots, rabbits, shrubs and mature trees. Penny Smith is working with a classteacher, the deputy headteacher, and two classes of children. Their focus is the development of children's literacy skills and the increase of home-school understanding in this area.

> I have found my involvement in this project both exciting and challenging. As each week passes I feel more secure about what I have to offer and more confident about what I hope we'll achieve and the ways in which we might do so. These first few months have been very important in laying a firm foundation for our future work together. I have needed time to clarify for myself and the school my new and dual role of practitioner and researcher.

> Initially it has seemed most appropriate to try to establish my role as another teacher in the classroom by fitting in with the normal classroom routine, working with the children and offering support and guidance in as many ways as possible. Gifts of 'big books', tapes, records have helped to indicate my desire to be useful and accepted. In a project of this nature it is obviously extremely important to gain the respect and trust of the school members — headteacher, staff and children. I am aware that the enthusiasm of the headteacher and class teacher for the project is matched by the guarded feelings of some of the other staff who, I believe, still question my motives. The

Figure 12: A father with his son on their first day in the nursery'

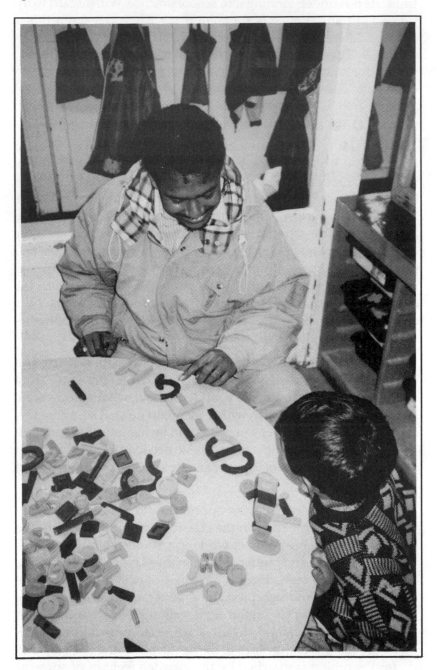

need to find ways of regularly informing the rest of the staff about the workings of the project is clearly going to be very important to our work.

Of particular importance is my relationship with the class teacher, which can be seen as a partnership between lecturer and teacher. She has a sound knowledge of the children, their parents and the community and therefore an understanding of what would be feasible and valuable in this particular school. We have needed time to build the mutual trust and co-oper-ation which will be essential if the project is to succeed. There may well be strong parallels here between the ways in which we do this and what we hope to achieve with parents. We both have to recognise the implicit rules we are developing for working together.

I see our partnership as a very important part of the project because I believe it will give the project credibility in the eyes of the teaching profession as well as other workers in the field. In order to influence practice and effect change there has to be a strong link with the 'grass roots'. The work of Donald Graves (1983) and Lucy Calkins (1983) has provided guidelines for my approach. As collaborative researchers they worked in close partnership with teachers in a class to bring about gradual change.

Our overall aim is to find ways of opening up a more genuine dialogue between teachers and parents about early literacy at home and in school. Misconceptions are common on both sides. Parents whose children are at the nursery class have expressed concern that their children spend all their time playing (often outside) and are hardly ever required to sit quietly at a table. Their view of school and its function is based on their own experiences as children. Teachers often have misconceived ideas about the literacy experiences of the home. Prejudices and low expectations are common and the blame for children's under-achievement is placed on factors outside the school. We have much to learn about the diverse experiences of the home, an understanding of which would enable us, together with parents, to identify the common links.

One way in which we aim to develop closer co-operation and understanding is through home visiting. The reasons for this are various — uncertainty about the value, the human resources needed to make it possible, the need for interpreters in order to communicate effectively with all parents, fear that some parents may feel that teachers are intruding. However, the classteacher and I are particularly enthusiastic about this aspect of our work. Hilary Minns (1990) recounts the clear value to be gained from such visits. She illustrates powerfully the ways in which her visits deepened her understanding of the children, their families and the variety of literacy experiences of the children.

In this project, we hope to have made a visit to each child's parents before the end of the Autumn term. It will be interesting not only to document the visits themselves, but also to analyse the advantages and disadvantages that may become apparent depending on who makes the first visit. The interest will come from informal discussions with the parents about their children (their hobbies, interests, literacy experiences). This discussion will then be summarised and written in the Primary Learning Record which is treated more fully in a later article (Barrs et al, 1988). One of the key features of this record is that it includes as an important element, two written summaries of a conference with parents, undertaken at the beginning and end of the school year. The formal record of these discussions speaks volumes about the respect the school has for the parent's knowledge of their own child — a knowledge which previously has been officially ignored in our professional records on children.

We hope that parents will welcome the opportunity not only to talk more freely in their own environment but also to have their knowledge documented. It will be important to ensure that the interpreters we use not only speak a language but also understand the underlying issues related to our view of home-school partnership.

Future visits throughout the year will focus on introducing a record of children's reading experiences at home through a home-school reading card. The school already has a policy of encouraging children to take books home to share with parents but at present provides no formal record. A priority will be to try to find how parents, whose first language is not English can

Figure 13: 'Asegul and Ruta listen to a recorded story'

be offered ways of communicating with the teachers. For instance, we may classify and number the various book-related activities that parents can do with children — talk about the story, discuss the pictures, read to your child, read with your child, and so on. These will be listed on a school 'book mark' card available in relevant languages. Parents, with children's help, may then choose simply to write the number corresponding to the activity. The system offers the beginnings of communication about reading support.

Regular analysis of the record cards will provide useful information about the reading interests of the children, the chosen 'book activities', and, for those parents who are able to give written responses, an indication of some of the concerns they have about early reading experiences. It is very likely that this aspect of the project will provide our research focus as we would like to build on previous work done by Peter Hannon and his team.

The initiatives described reflect our aims to find out more about literacy at home. In order to provide a balance, we plan in the spring and summer terms to make a video of children engaged in some of the range of purposeful literacy experiences in the nursery school. We will send copies home so that parents and children can discuss the content. The videos might also provide useful material for a wider audience, for instance, students and staff at The University of Greenwich.

I believe that children's learning can be greatly enhanced if parents and teachers have a shared understanding of how children organise and go about their learning at home and at school. I feel the project has begun to set up important opportunities for the development of a genuine dialogue between home and school.

School Two: a primary school (for children aged 5-11)

The school is surrounded by rented housing dating from the 1900s through to recent times. It occupies a small triangle of land bounded by three busy major roads. The areas has an uncared-for appearance, and there is clear evidence of systematic vandalism.

There are 344 children attending the school. Traditionally, it has served a mainly white (English, Scottish and Irish) catchment area, but since the 1970s, Bangladeshi, Caribbean, Chinese and Somali families have moved into the area. As in many other multicultural, inner city areas subject to population change and movement, there has sometimes been suspicion and tension between culturally different groups. Some children bring unfavourable attitudes to school which can spill over in both the playground and the class-room. The school is seeking solutions to these issues by means of the curriculum.

Florence Beetlestone is working with a classteacher, a science co-ordinator and a class of six year-old children. Their focus is the development of portable science packs that can move between school and home and promote discussion and understanding of learning in science. The children are involved in the design of the packs and will play an important part in initiating parental comment when materials are in their homes.

Here are Florence's experiences and thoughts:

My first visit to the school confirmed my view that it was the right school for me to work in. I felt extremely comfortable. Everyone was very supportive and the children were responsive and eager to learn. The classteacher was an excellent choice and I knew immediately that we would work well together. Neither of us really knew, on my first couple of visits, how the project would eventually work out, but we were full of enthusiasm to try.

We both saw the importance of taking a 'low key' approach. I had to adjust my role. I've been used to having a fairly high status in schools when I visit my students as supervising tutor. It seemed particularly important to establish a different role, as I want essentially to act as a catalyst to enable the school to take on change when I leave. Lessons learnt from the Haringay Reading Project (Tizard et al, 1982) showed how important it would be that ways of working continued after the project worker withdrew.

In September 1990 we worked out a rough plan for the year. The first term would be one which grounded the project, establishing relationships, patterns of working and research angles. The second term would involve 'formal' contact with parents to set up discussion about the science packs. This would be continued during part of the third term when we also plan to

Figure 14: 'Setting up the candle experiment'

set up a number of feedback sessions for the school staff.. Our plans need to be woven around the annual SATS (Standard Assessment Tasks taken by all English seven-year olds) that some of the children have to do towards the end of the year. We want to introduce the idea of 'science packs' as a means of sharing ideas with parents.

Initially, I have got to know the class. Part of adopting the low key role means that ideas need to come from the 'grass roots', particularly the children, rather than from outside the school. Therefore I have established myself with the class as a regular teacher who comes in every week on Tuesday on science projects. I have been able to build up trust and confidence with them in this way. It hasn't taken long. At the end of the second week a visiting teacher asked who I was and the children told him, 'It's alright, she comes on Tuesday,' I hoped that parents would hear of me through the children in this natural way. When it comes to developing ideas with them I will have some credibility as a teacher in their children's school.

Figure 15: 'Watching the candle experiment'

To date we have done three sessions on the theme of 'forces'. This has helped us see how the children work on science, build up relationships with them and begin to talk to them about their ideas of science.

In my third week I watched a candle experiment which had been set up with six children. The group were very interested; they observed well and were able to describe what was happening — 'The candle's gone out, the water's rising!'. They appeared to have some understanding of the forces involved in the movement of the water, and some ideas that the air inside the jar was being displaced. I took photographs of each stage so that we could pursue their thinking further.

My plans are to use the photographs in discussion, so as to find out about what they had thought might happen; whether they could sequence the process; and discuss whether sequence was important in order to find out if they could explain what had happened and why. Most importantly, could they draw any overall conclusions about the experiment which might help them to formulate some of the underlying reasons for the way in which the forces operated?

The children have shown considerable interest in the work and some expressed a wish to take science equipment and books home to show their parents. For many parents science is an unknown part of the school curriculum, so they often lack confidence to give support to their children. However, when the books came back to school they showed evidence of parents having helped children to record the science activities and 'findings' in writing and drawings. This gave us enormous pleasure, as it moved the project on in a very positive way, but also meant that parental involvement in science had been initiated naturally by the children.

Recently, following up on this success, we held an open afternoon for parents to come to school and to get involved in science activities with the children. The children had written letters of invitation and this resulted in high attendance. We took particular care to provide a friendly atmosphere, offering cups of tea and welcoming younger siblings. The afternoon was such a success that we are planning another in a few weeks' time.

At this early stage in the project we already feel (with the children's help), that we have been able to reassure a number of parents that science is grounded in our everyday lives and events. In addition, given the children's enthusiasm, we are now ready to enlist their help in the production of more substantial packs.

School Three: a primary school (for children aged 5- 11)

The school is housed in an old London 'Board School' on the Isle of Dogs, a fast-growing city redevelopment area. The neighbourhood has recently undergone rapid and striking change. Old Victorian and pre-second World War rented housing now sits conspicuously alongside partially sold apartment developments aimed at the commercial and professional staff on the relocated businesses of Docklands.

There are 283 children on the school list. Traditionally, this is an area where white (English, Irish and Scottish) families were

66

very much in the majority. Recent years have seen a steady growth in the Bangladeshi, Chinese, Caribbean and Vietnamese communities. It is possible to find evidence in the neighbourhood (eg. graffiti, verbal comments from children and adults) of unwelcoming attitudes towards the newly arrived groups. The school is particularly concerned to promote caring and understanding attitudes amongst children.

Geoff Sheath is working with a classteacher and a class of 30 eleven-year olds. Small groups of children are developing mathematical topics and recording them on video tape. Copies will be made and children will be able to take them home to share with their parents. Geoff and the classteacher will set up close liaison with parents to follow up with further discussion and comments.

Geoff gives the following account of his experiences and thoughts:

London's Docklands is a curiously mixed area. Ten years ago it was terribly depressed economically. My few visits left me with the feeling of an area falling apart. Although the insides of the flats I visited were often very nice, the dereliction and petty vandalism that characterised the outside and public areas spoke to me of working-class communities falling apart as opportunities for employment evaporated. Over the next ten years I had little contact with Docklands. Once or twice I took my own children up to London on the new Docklands Light Railway and watched as futuristic new commercial buildings sprouted. I knew that a growing amount of public housing in Docklands was let to tenants from ethnic minorities.

So when I discovered the school that I was to work in was at the heart of Docklands I was very curious about what I would find. In the event, it has been a revelation. Physically it has one aspect of the area at each of its four sides: local authority housing on one side, inter-war private housing on the next, almost complete new housing on a third and industrial premises on the fourth.

Then there is the staff. For someone who spends much of his time training teachers, going into school can be quite a testing and thankless event. If you have no difficulties then you get no credit, if you do have difficulties then people always knew that teacher educators only do the job because they can't teach

Figure 16: 'Geoff working with a group on algebra'

children. I actually enjoy teaching children and I think that has helped me to be accepted when I work in schools. But in the past I have also often been welcomed because I brought expertise which I could use and share. Not so much in this school. The staff are dauntingly aware and involved, and have the expertise to translate ideas into action. In the half-term that I have been in the school, for example, they have had two public receptions to launch schemes funded by industry, and are at the point of holding a complete day's course to share with other schools their expertise in information technology, charging £30 per head.

In the area of parental involvement too, the school has a good record of using a number of techniques. This means that being involved with the project is not terribly special — they have been involved in others. However, parental involvement in education can always be revisited and improved upon, particularly in a culturally diverse neighbourhood. Furthermore, I will be concentrating on the use of video, something which staff and children haven't developed to any great extent.

Gaining confidence has been a major task of mine during the first half term and will continue to be so throughout the project. The teacher I am working with is very talented. He has asked me to do algebra activities with the class, and I have taught a series of one-off lessons to do with groups. These have generally been productive with the children, until last week when I completely misjudged their ability. My success in gaining the confidence of children is difficult to assess. I am a novelty to some, to others a positive figure.

The issue of confidence is difficult but crucial. Most educational research has to take seriously the issue of access and one of the key factors to obtaining access is to gain the confidence of the other people involved. Confidence covers several aspects of interaction. First the participants must feel that they get something out of the process. This could be kudos or interest, or it might be just a warm feeling of 'being of service'. Teachers and other education professionals are often amenable to the latter reward, but in this case we have also been able to offer some tangible assets, like access to some funding and human resources.

With regard to the children, I am expecting the kudos and interest associated with video- making to be the main rewards. However, I recognise that once the pattern of my weekly visit is established they could come to look forward to my presence. For the parents, like the children, the reward I envisage is largely one of interest, interest in their children's achievements. I know from preliminary conversations that many families have their own video recorders, particularly the Bangladeshi community for whom Hindi films are very popular with the whole family. So videos have high status and I hope this carries over to the tapes made by children.

A second aspect of confidence is that of integrity, more particularly that people are dealt with honestly and in a way that shows respect. To date, it has been easier to establish this with the classteacher than with the children. As far as the parents are concerned, it might be best if I enable and support the classteacher rather than become directly involved myself. I shall feel my way on this.

Having established myself as an interesting, but maybe marginal, figure in the first half of the term I now have to move towards a more focused role for the rest of this term. My aim will be first to introduce the idea of a video of the school from pupils' view-points and then to work steadily, week by week, with small groups to plan, write scripts, video and edit the results. Up until now I have worked entirely in the classroom, which has helped me to become reasonably accepted. In future I propose to work in a number of locations with various video groups. This is partly to minimise any disruption in class for the class teacher but also to give a student teacher (not from my own institution) space for her teaching practice with the class.

In the summer term the class is spending a week at a camping site in Bayeux. This offers a wonderful opportunity for the children to use their acquired skills to record the experience for their parents. Also, we can take copies of our 'school' and 'maths' videos to give to a partner school in Normandy.

Despite a preparedness to link with 'opportunistic' developments like the French trip, I still feel the heart of the project is the maths videos that the children will be making in the next half term. We will surely encounter some difficulty because I am in for only half a day a week. However, given my developing relationships with the class teacher and children, I feel confident that I will quickly reach a point where some children will use video as an alternative way of recording classroom activities and events. An activity of relevance to the project will thus be continuing to develop in my absence.

I hope that early in the Spring term we will begin sending maths videos home with children for family viewing and that home-school contact to discuss these — with interpreters if necessary — will begin before Easter.

At the time of writing I feel the project has made a very effective start. Involvement and goodwill is developing well in the school and I now feel significantly more integrated and confident about my role and contribution.

Overview

In writing about our experiences, we have tried to give very open accounts of the process of establishing ourselves as collaborators with teachers, children and parents. Traditionally, project workers have not always included such details in their writing. They tend to see them as untidy and unreportable. The decision to give them a high profile in this chapter reflects our belief that they hold a central place in the project's progress at this moment. They are of fundamental importance to the 'preparation of the ground'. Four shared themes can be found in our writing.

First, we lay great emphasis on trust-building and relationship-making with children and class teachers. This calls for a pre-paredness to play down our higher education 'mantle' and accept that we are working in a context where new roles have to be negotiated and professional confidence and expertise re-established. There is little doubt that the project's original aim of getting support and resources to class teachers is in fact a complex and subtle process demanding considerable skill from outsiders.

Second, at this early stage, we put all our energies into develo-ping the curriculum ideas. This has left little time for reflection and 'research' apart from the entries in our diaries and the recording of all discussion about the project. School research that is instigated by outsiders can be an intrusive activity. We therefore feel it im-portant to focus on helping and teaching, as we want the school to feel assured of our worth and commitment. Classrooms are places where children make constant high demands on teachers' energy. Understandably, class teachers have little time for those who stand away from the action.

Third, we identify with the slow and careful pace of the project during this early phase. It gives essential time for familiarisation and adjustment and it recognises that the projects needs time to make the journey from the classroom to the parents. It is essential that all are on board — teachers, children and lecturers. This cannot be rushed.

Lastly, in her writing, Penny highlights the important parallel between the class teacher/lecturer partnership and the profes-sional/parent partnership that is to follow. This is a key theme and it goes to the core of our notion of 'preparing the ground'. If we as professionals can show each other a high degree of openess, trust, honesty and goodwill, this will surely put us in a strong positiom to establish meaningful links with parents.

Bibliography

Barrs M. *et al* (1988) *The Primary Language Record*. London: Centre for Language in Primary Education

Calkins, L. (1983) *Lessons From a Child*. London: Heinemann

Graves, D.H. (1983) *Writing: Teachers and Childen at Work*. London: Heinemann

Tizard, J. Schofield, W. and Hewison, J. (1992) Collaboration between teachers and parents in assisting children's reading. *Br. Jr. and Ed. Psychology.* Vol .52, No.1, 1-15

It is no secret that in many countries the children of the rural poor seem to have the least experience of early literacy and to suffer the consequences of slow beginnings in reading and writing. The contexts and texts of urban, schooled reading are not part of their environment. Where this is the case, the role of the nursery school becomes even more important, and the school, as a location, brings together those who have a regard for the children' s first steps in reading and writing. In a situation quite different from those described in earlier chapters, we see how insightful teachers respond to the children's under-standings and intentions. They also create a social context where the parents can share the children's obvious enjoy-ment of pictures, stories and writing. The final texts are noteworthy as they demonstrate how parents, teachers and children come to appreciate the nature and functions of literacy in the modern world. As a result, we shall all have to examine much more closely our expectations of families whose traditions of literacy are different from those of teachers, especially now that television has extended all children's vision of the world beyond the boundaries of their home environment.

Chapter 5

LEARNING TO READ AT NURSERY SCHOOL

*Maria Luisa Gil, Maria Paz Ortega,
Maria Pilar Retuerto*

The Scenarios: The Children and the Classes

Our interest in boys and girls at nursery school learning to read in a lively, untraumatic way led us to pioneer the experiment 'Learning to read at nursery school'. Motivated by Dr Cohen's work 'Learning to Read Early' and by our contact with Dr. Gloria Medrano in conferences and congresses on Pre-school Education, in the academic year 1985-1986, we started the reading experiment with the smallest children, encouraged and guided by Carmen Garcia Colmenares, lecturer in Developmental and Educational Psychology at Palencia Teacher Training College.

We began to work in our own classrooms, two of which are in a neighbourhood in the outskirts of the city with a poor socio-cultural environment and a high unemployment rate, taking in children with emotional and physical handicaps such as Down's Syndrome and speech problems. The third class is in a rural environment in a predominantly agricultural town with a low to medium socio-cultural level, attended by school children from the neighbouring villages.

There are about 20 pupils in each of the three classes, although in the rural centre some boys and girls start at five years of age instead of the usual four. The reason for this delay in starting is that in our country, pre-school education is neither free nor compulsory, so families in outlying villages can't cope with the problems of transport and a school meal.

During these last few years we have been working with four and five year olds, endeavouring to start the learning/teaching of reading in a continuous and progressive way, very slowly at first, more systematically in the second pre-school year. Each teacher has stayed with the same children for the two years.

Our fundamental objectives were:

- To improve the aptitudes and skills of the children from low socio-cultural backgrounds, thus trying to eliminate failure at school, as far as possible.

- To prove the importance of early learning in any subject, especially written language, in order to develop the cognitive, affective and social skills of our infants.

- To enable the family to gain easier access to the school environment so that right from the beginning they can reinforce the acquisition of reading and writing skills in their children in a lively, pleasant way.

Development of the Experiment

We set out from the premise that the written message should permeate the classroom, so it was set out to create an 'atmosphere of literacy'. We used a series of hand-written cards which we fixed to the walls, windows and tables. This enabled the children to identify objects with their corresponding written symbol. In part our intention was to ensure that the children were not deprived of the written word, since in the world outside they are exposed to it: in the baker's, and on the wrappers of the sweets they eat. Besides, their favourite characters in stories and on television have names the children recognise which identify them and differentiate them from the rest.

The first reading cards the children are given at age four correspond to their name and age and then they are introduced to cards referring to classroom objects, and subjects dealt with in class

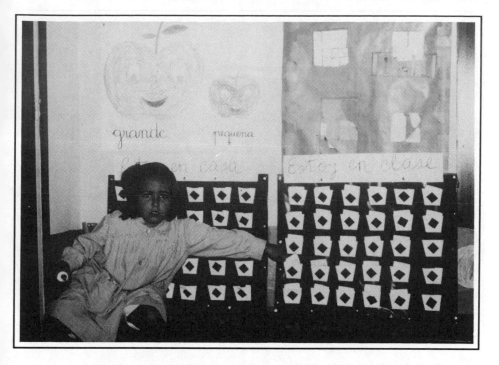

Figure 17: 'Laura is in class'

sessions, such as the days of the week and the weather. The first cards they handle, bearing their own names and those of their classmates, are presented in a vivid way by means of attendance slips 'I'm in class'/I'm at home', so they get to know their own name and those of their classmates. In the first picture below, Laura puts her card on the 'I'm in class' index. The names of the girls and boys who are not at school that day are put on the 'I'm at home' index. Cards with 'Good morning', 'Good afternoon', the day of the week, the weather, such as 'sunny' or 'misty,' are put up at the beginning of every school day.

Also, games are played in which the children have to recognise words which begin and end in the same way. They also have to look for short and long words, share classmates' names, change around the names of classroom objects, check to see if all the cards have been put in the right places. Has 'windows' been written on the door, for example, or 'chair' on the table?

These card games are played during the first term, until January. Later, we start on discrimination of sounds and phonemes The

Figure 18: 'It's Tuesday and it's sunny'

children begin to pick out the vowels which appear on the different cards, in their names, or in words which they suggest to us. Vowels are identified by their sound and graphics and once these are known the consonant phonemes are introduced.

Activities involved in the decoding of phonemes include:

- looking for cards beginning and ending with a particular sound,
- looking for cards containing a particular sound
- Activities related to the graphic realisation of the sound being studied, using finger-painting and materials such as sand and wax.

In the following year, at age five, besides reinforcing aspects ingrained in the children earlier, reading and writing are tackled simultaneously in a contextualised way. As well as using the cards, the teachers start working with written texts and stories which are simple but of interest to our pre-school infants. We try to find books

Figure 19: 'A card game to cover different parts of the body'

and stories which are written with the same cursive lettering as we use on the cards.

The activities become more and more complex, enabling us to observe the development of the psycholinguistic skills and competence of our pupils. Some of these, graded in terms of increasing difficulty, might be:

- Associating words and drawings
- Ordering jumbled words so they make a meaningful sentence
- Forming a sentence starting with one word only
- Changing a word in a sentence
- Drawing what is represented graphically in a sentence.
- Writing a sentence about what is suggested in a drawing
- Dictation of words or sentences.

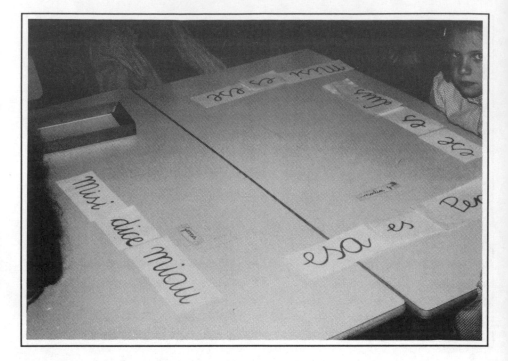

Figure 20: 'Making up sentences about story characters'

At the end of the pre-school stage reading comprehension is well developed in boys and girls, even in those who show some kind of problem such as speech abnormalities or hyperactivity. At the same time the children's production of writing is also outstanding: they write short narratives, stories and at the time of the Mayoral election in the local villages, one class even produced a newspaper.

Reading in the Family

In order to get the families to participate and collaborate with us in their children's education, particularly their reading, we get in touch with parents at the beginning of each school year to explain our method of teaching reading and writing. The official curricula issued by administrative bodies in education do not include the teaching of written language to pre-school children.

At these meetings and throughout the school year, we try to convey to mothers and fathers the importance of reading at home and how to keep up the practice. We give them similar directives

Figure 21: 'Our electoral campaign — a page from the class newspaper'

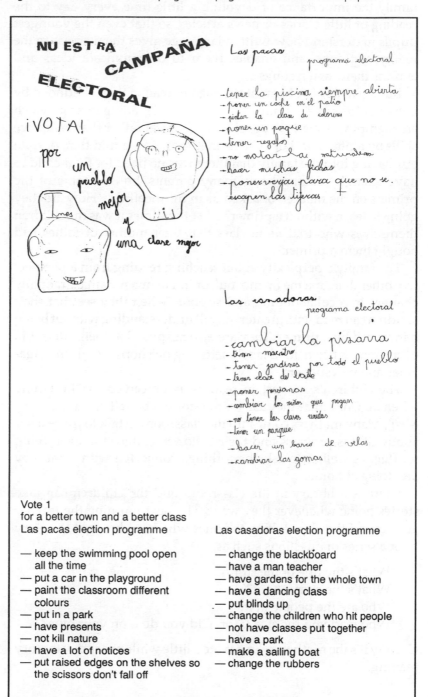

Vote 1
for a better town and a better class
Las pacas election programme

— keep the swimming pool open
  all the time
— put a car in the playground
— paint the classroom different
  colours
— put in a park
— have presents
— not kill nature
— have a lot of notices
— put raised edges on the shelves so
  the scissors don't fall off

Las casadoras election programme

— change the blackboard
— have a man teacher
— have gardens for the whole town
— have a dancing class
— put blinds up
— change the children who hit people
— not have classes put together
— have a park
— make a sailing boat
— change the rubbers

to those we give the children in the classroom. We point out to the family the importance of devoting a little time every day to the reading of little stories or news articles, so that even the youngest pupils understand how written language gives them access to the reality of things, and enables them to communicate ideas and express their own feelings.

But the majority of parents learned to read in their childhood by means of 'primers': totally decontexualised reading texts in which an attempt was made to develop mechanical rather than reflective skills by alphabetical or syllabic methods. So we find that, despite our having told the family that there was no need for their child to have a single reading book, many parents, bought some of the primers on the market, or asked us in the meetings: 'How are they going to learn without a primer?'. At other times it was the children themselves who told us in class that their mother or father had bought them a primer.

The family's perplexity about teaching reading from a perspective other than 'ma me mi mo mu', or 'mi mama me ama' gradually changes into collaboration and support when they see that their children can read with greater overall understanding without being hammered by a primer. They are also surprised at their interest in everything written: food labels, lettering on shops, words in magazines and newspapers.

The children's interest in reading is perceived by the family when for Christmas they ask for the stories about 'Pepa and her cat Misi'. Many mothers come into the classroom to talk to the teacher about all this progress and their children's interest in everything written, as well as to ask about things connected with what they are doing at home.

There is a library in the classroom and the children can take stories home whenever they want. The next morning the teacher goes round the class asking the ones who have brought the story back a series of questions such as:

'What's the title of the story?'
'What's the story about?'
'Who are the people in it?"
'Who read you the story?' or 'Did you do it on your own?'

Usually it's the mothers who devote a little while every day to story reading.

The best anecdote about the children's interest in reading is the case of a girl called Izaskun who was always wanting Friday to come round, the day when her mother would buy her a story which the teacher then read to the class. At the end of the year the mother donated the whole collection of stories to the school, hoping that as they had been so useful to her daughter, they might serve to encourage other children.

Another way of encouraging families to collaborate with us in the reading was to arrange for children to take their own stories and writings home. Also, seeing their children's drawings and writings in the school magazine edited by the parents, enabled families to follow their children's progress and at the same time eliminated their fears about our system of teaching them how to read. On page 84 is one such story by Diego aged 5.

Conclusions

After more than six years' work trying to develop the interest of our four and five year-olds in written language, we can conclude by saying that:

- It is possible to teach pre-school children to read in an understanding and lively way, as long as one takes the children's centres of interest as a starting point. The use of children's stories allows even the youngest to develop a capacity for overall comprehension of what they are reading in context, since what they read makes sense and gives them knowledge of 'something previously hidden'. We consider it more suitable to use texts which tell stories rather than the classic 'primers' which take an alphabetical and syllabic approach. This does not mean that we do not consider the decoding of phonemes and sounds important, but that this should always be done through games and activities which stimulate an interest in the written message. In the words of Dr. Medrano, we need to promote 'learning to read with enjoyment'.

- Reading at the pre-school stage becomes a necessity and a social obligation when working with girls and boys from low socio-cultural backgrounds, since reading difficulties in the first years of primary education are one of the major causes of failure at school. One has therefore to seek the collaboration of the family, so that they understand the

Figure 22: 'Diego's story'

Mariano va a patinar y sube a la montaña, baja muy deprisa y se asusta porque se va a caer a un lago al fin se cae

diego albariz

y su creatividad

Mariano goes skateboarding and climbs up the mountain. He goes down very fast and gets frightened because he's going to fall in a lake. At the end he falls.

Diego Albariz

and his creativity

importance of success at school in the early years and recognise how important it is that the children see that their family is helping them. In this respect, we should point out that the collaboration of the family has been very important and positive, as we have observed an avid interest in the children's progress through school from the nursery stage on.

- The methodology used has proved highly suitable, enabling us to develop a series of skills in the children such as: capacity for observation, analytical perception, memory, an earlier deciphering of links between speaking and writing, strengthening of metacognitive thinking, greater autonomy in reading comprehension and in initiation into writing.

- Finally, the teachers' role is more gratifying because the use of a methodology rooted in a particular context compels teachers to use strategies based on the interests and needs of the children and not on a routine curriculum or impersonal reading primer. Our everyday problems forced us to re-examine our working practices, to be more aware of what we were doing, and to develop strategies which would enable our boys and girls to make steady progress.

References

Cohen, R. (1977) *L'Apprentissage Precoce de la Lecture*, Paris: PUF

Medrano, G. (1984) 'Preparacion de un ambiente enriquecido en el aula de pre escolar' 1 *Jornadas Nacionales de Educacion Pre escolar Málaga*, pp. 17-21

Stenhouse, L. (1975) *An Introduction to Curriculum Research and Development*, London: Heinemann

Tonucci, F. (1976) *A Tre Anni Si Fa Ricerca*, Firenze: Lib. Ed. Fiorentina

In the last two decades we have come to realise that, in all languages, the ways of describing children's entry into the written word are changing. Literacy is no longer understood as an absolute term; it is a relative one. We acknowledge the complexity of the social contexts and practices for literacy which the young have to learn about, both at school and in the world outside it. Slowly, we are also becoming aware that so-called objective tests cannot give, in a single operation, a full account of children's progress nor of their difficulties. In order to be faithful to our growing understandings we are looking for other ways to describe children's development as writers and readers. By using the conventions of ethnography we are now able to admit different kinds of evidence. This next chapter describes The Primary Language Record. This is a way of reporting on children's reading behaviours, attitudes and understandings of the texts they read as they are reading them. This way of recording reading brings together the words of the parents, the children and the teachers as they reflect together on how they observe and describe the learners' progress. First devised and pioneered in London, this Record is in use in many places in England and in North America.

Chapter 6

THE PRIMARY LANGUAGE RECORD: CHILDREN, PARENTS AND TEACHERS WORKING AND LEARNING TOGETHER

Helen James and Margaret Wyeth

Over the past five years we have been involved in the development and use of the Primary Language Record, an observation-based system of record keeping for children aged three to eleven. As teachers with substantial experience of the Primary Language Record, we aim to show in this article how its use in our classrooms has helped a great deal in providing continuity in language and literacy development between home and school for children and in promoting home-school dialogue. We have been able to find out about, and to build on, the experiences, knowledge and understanding that children bring from home, through our use of the PLR. The children are not treated as blank sheets when they arrive in school.

We will look at the aims and structures of the Primary Language Record for involving parents and children. We will also look at how we have implemented the Record in our classrooms and schools and at the effect this has had in terms of classroom organisation and of overall school policies. Then we will look in some detail at examples of parent/teacher and parent/child discussions and show how they have helped us in supporting children's language and literacy development.

The Primary Language Record has been designed as a framework for record-keeping for children from 3-11. The Record is divided into two sections. The first provides teachers with a framework for observing children's language and literacy development through keeping diaries and more detailed samples. The second part forms the child's official school record and includes the parent and child conferences, and also a summary by the class teacher of the child's progress and development. Both parts involve all staff who teach the child at school. As has already been implied however, we propose in this article to focus on the crucial roles played by parents and children in this structure.

The PLR was developed by teachers, advisory teachers and inspectors working together and was piloted in 50 London schools in 1986-7. Now it is widely used across London, in other areas of England and Wales, and in parts of the United States. It is only in the last few years that teachers have seen the value of listening to parents and learning from them, and the PLR has been a part of that development. Parents know a great deal about their children's development and about the literacy experiences their children have had. Hence the principles behind the Record include *the involvement of parents and the involvement of children*. This involvement is formally included in the Record through twice-yearly discussions, called 'conferences' between teachers and parents and between teachers and children.

Parent Conferences

The 'Primary Language Record Handbook', which gives guidance on using the Record, explains the purposes of the parent conferences:

> *The purpose of the discussion between parent(s) and teacher is to encourage a two-way communication between home and school, to let parent(s) share their knowledge of the child, at home and at school, their observations and concerns, hopes and expectations. Regular informal conversations between parents and teachers can help to establish a real partnership between home and school and can create*

a forum where achievements as well as concerns can be discussed. '
(p.12)

Parents are invited to come and have a discussion with their child's class teacher some time during the Autumn term, with a further optional discussion towards the end of the school year in the Summer term. A summary of the discussions is recorded on the main Record, which then forms part of the child's official school record. Usually these discussions last for about 15 minutes and they can be arranged at a time most suitable to parents and teachers.

Both of our London schools had a tradition of 'parents' evenings' held in the Autumn term, but these meetings between parents and teachers could often be rather a vague conversation, where the teachers said they hadn't really had time to get to know the child yet but that they seemed to be settling down fairly well. The change to using the PLR affected our practice in several ways. First, the fact that a summary of the main points of the conversation is written down, made a difference to teachers and parents, giving the discussion greater status. This meant that teachers and parents made more efforts to ensure that they actually met. Open evenings had usually been on one or two evenings only, and if the parents were unable to come, little effort was made to see them at other times.

Now many schools, including our own, are more flexible in the times that they offer to parents. Many offer appointments during the school day for those parents not at work, and appointments just before or just after school when parents come to pick their children up. This flexibility by schools has been matched by more enthusiasm from parents:

> 'I think the school itself has got quite a good response where open evenings are concerned, because there is that communication between teachers and parents and it's written down. I think that's important. I know quite a few of the parents down the school and they like the participation that parents have ' (Catherine Hayes, mother of 3 children at Harrington Hill School)

Parents' status at the conferences is now greater. They come to the conference as experts on their own child's language and literacy: they have information about the child's behaviour at home, about the child's interests and knowledge, which teachers now recognise as valuable.

At the conferences, we had to make sure that we enabled parents to feel relaxed and confident enough to talk openly about their child's achievements, and about any difficulties. The type of questions we asked parents was important: 'Does your child enjoy reading at home?' was almost certain to be answered with a 'yes', whatever the reality of the situation! Open-ended questions, that didn't imply a particular answer, were very important and teachers have got together to work out the best ways of asking questions of this kind. The ways in which parents were treated in the school generally were also important in encouraging parents to feel that we really wanted to learn from them. After having used the Record for several years we have found that parents now come to the conferences ready with things they want to tell us about their child.

It is clearly very important that bilingual parents feel welcomed into the school and know that their child's language and culture will be respected and valued in school. The conferences provide an opportunity for teachers to find out which languages the child uses and with whom, and also what the language(s) are of the home and the community. Where the school is not able to provide a bilingual teacher to interpret, parents who are not experienced in using English are encouraged to bring along a relative, older sibling, or a friend to interpret. We don't just rely on sending notes home to invite parents to these conferences. We ask the children to invite their parents to the school, or speak to parents when they come to collect their children.

Child Conferences

In this way parents' observations become part of the main Record. The conference with the child allows the child's opinions also to be an important part of the Record. This, too, lasts about 15 minutes, although it can vary with individual children. Again, open-ended questions are necessary to give the child the opportunity to talk openly and honestly about themselves and their learning. How effective this is will be influenced by the way of working in the classroom:

> *A language and literacy conference is designed to give the child an opportunity to talk about and discuss with the teacher her/his experiences, achievements and interests as a language user. A conference like this should be a continuation of an already existing dialogue between child and teacher and a means of establishing, in a more*

structured way, children's view of themselves as language learners and language users in and outside school. It should also encourage the child to play an increasingly active part in her/his own learning and provide regular opportunities to reflect on progress. (P.L.R. Handbook p.14)

Obviously much organisation and thought are involved in enabling the teacher to spend 15 minutes with each child in the class for the conference. Schools have tackled this in different ways. When we introduced conferences into our schools, teachers felt they could only do the child conferences when the rest of the class wasn't there, or when another adult had control of the rest of the class. This was done by using assembly times, play times and times when another teacher could take the class for singing, or for a story. However, as teachers and children became more accustomed to these conferences, teachers have found it possible to incorporate individual discussions into the general classroom routine. This has meant considering how the classroom is organised. The children need to know how to work as independently as possible within the classroom, and the teacher needs to pick the best moments to work with an individual child. Children relish this attention and see the conference as an important time with their teacher. The day after a 5 year old had had a conference with Margaret she remarked 'Can you do me again today?' Teachers who were initially sceptical about the huge amount of time involved have discovered that the information that they got, as well as the positive effect on the child's self-esteem, have certainly made the organisational effort worthwhile.

How the Conferences Help Teachers Support Children's Development

In this section we will look at how particular conferences have both enhanced home/school dialogue and helped support the child's literacy development by improved school provision. The first example is a white monolingual English-speaking girl, who started school in 1989, aged 5. The conferences were carried out several weeks after she started school.

This child was clearly a fluent reader before she started school. Her parents were initially concerned that this fact would not be picked up by her teachers, which would impede her development. During Natalie's first week in school Margaret, one of the authors

Figure 23: 'Record of conferences with Natalie and her parents at the beginning of the school year'.

Primary Language Record

School _____ School Year

Name **Natalie**	DoB _____ Summer born child ___
	☐ Boy ☐ Girl

Languages understood	Languages read
Languages spoken	Languages written

Details of any aspects of hearing, vision or coordination affecting the child's language/literacy. Give the source and date of this information.	Names of staff involved with child's language and literacy development.

Part A To be completed during the Autumn Term

A1 Record of discussion between child's parent(s) and class teacher *(Handbook pages 12-13)*

Always shown an interest in books (since a baby). Had many books read to her by mum and dad (anyone who'd read to her!!) Enjoys animal/nature books. Loves drawing and enjoys music. Readily writes stories at home. N. is obviously fluent at reading and her parents are concerned that this should be realised and noted by new teachers etc.

Signed Parent(s) _____ Teacher _____

Date _____

A2 Record of language/literacy conference with child *(Handbook pages 14-15)* I learned to read when I was three. My mummy pointed to the words and I tried to read. My favourite book is Jungle Book. The best story I've ever written is about a white elephant. I wrote it ages ago at home. My best writing in school has been my register. My writing is good and my reading. My mummy thinks I read very well too.

Date _____

of this article, had an informal chat with Natalie's mum, saying that she was very impressed by her fluency as a reader. In Margaret's classroom, the children read first thing in the morning every day, and she observes and records comments not only about the children she reads with, but also about other reading going on in the classroom. From these observations and from spending time reading with Natalie, she could quickly discover her reading abilities. This was important for Natalie's development as a reader, but it also meant that her parents felt more confident in the school. When it came to the parent conference her parents knew that the important information about their child's experiences and abilities would be received favourably by the school. All of this positive co-operation is in stark contrast to M. Clark's study in 1976 in Scotland, where she looked at a group of children similar to Natalie, in that they started school as fluent readers.

> *Few of the parents informed the school initially; their embarrassment at their children's early fluency making them reticent. Indeed several children sat quietly for several months without revealing their skill... The embarrassment of these parents and their diffidence at reporting their child's abilities, and the rebuff which some met when they did, seem matters of concern... Though one should not minimise the problems that these early fluent readers present in the classroom, it is important to stress that they are indeed the end of a continuum and may therefore highlight problems faced by many children on starting school.* ' (pp.55-6)

After these conferences, Margaret encouraged Natalie's interest in animal and nature books by talking about the class project on bears and asking her to choose some books about bears from the school library. Natalie also brought in a bear book from home. Natalie chose some of her favourite illustrations and these were photocopied to make an information book about bears, written by Natalie. She took on the style of information writing very well:

> *Panda bears come from China*
> *They eat bamboo shoots.*
> *I have seen one at the zoo.*
> *Koalas climb trees.*
> *They carry their babies on their backs.*
> *Polar bears live in the Arctic and they eat fish*
> *He is white so he can't be seen*

Figure 24: 'Record of conferences with Wing and his parents at the end of the school year'.

Part C <small>To be completed during the Summer Term*</small>   <small>*(Handbook page 35)*</small>

C1 Comments on the record by child's parent(s) His mum and his sister think that he likes reading a lot. He always likes someone to read to him when he gets home. His writing is now clearer. His maths is not bad, he enjoys that as well. He likes drawing too.

C2 Record of language/literacy conference with child My favourite thing in school is reading. I like Cat Sat On the Mat and Not Now Bernard. I can read some books now. I couldn't when I started. My sister teaches me to read. At home I speak Chinese. I get muddled sometimes in English. I like maths. I do lots of adding and taking away at home with my sister. I think my writing is really good now. My best writing is Cat Sat On The Mat. I typed it with my sister. At school I like playing 'had' with Daniel and Gurdeep.

C3 Information for receiving teacher
This section is to ensure that information for the receiving teacher is as up to date as possible. Please comment on changes and development in any aspect of the child's language since Part B was completed.

What experiences and teaching have helped/would help development? Record outcomes of any discussion with head teacher, other staff, or parent(s).

Signed: Parent(s) _____   Class Teacher _____

Date _____   Head Teacher _____

*To be completed by the Summer half-term for 4th year juniors.

I stayed in America.
Bears come from America.
Baloo comes from the jungle.
The End.

Natalie is now 8 years old. Her most recent parent conference shows her to be an enthusiastic reader, enjoying Roald Dahl novels, a Children's Bible, and carrying out simple experiments using ideas from books. In the child conference Natalie adds that she sometimes likes to read 'easy reads', enjoying some of her old favourites. This is clearly a picture of a child who has a wide range of reading interests and experiences and who is being enabled to build on all of this both at home and at school.

The second example is a bilingual child, whose languages are Cantonese and English. He started Nursery school in 1989, aged 3. His parents speak Cantonese and very little English and did not attend the first conference, and Wing would not speak at all to his teacher. He entered Margaret's class aged 5. These are the conference records at the end of a year in her class.

These conferences show a change from when he first started, in that his sister, aged 15, was able to come and interpret for his parents. Wing's own confidence in talking to adults has also greatly developed. His teachers know more about what goes on in his home and his family know more about what is going on in school. There is a link between his home and school experiences. Clearly, during the time that Wing was silent in the Nursery class, he was not only developing his understanding of English but also learning a great deal about literacy. His teacher noted at the time in his PLR diary:

'Wing likes books and is often in the book corner. He chatters to the books but will stop if an adult comes anywhere near him.'

The important adults in his literacy development have been not only his teachers in school, but also his parents, and particularly his 15 year old sister who reads with him in English every night. As he says, 'my sister teaches me to read.' Although his parents are not literate in English it is clear from the conferences that they are very supportive of his literacy development. Their presence at the conferences has coincided with his increased confidence and literacy skills.

Wing is now 6. His mother has said, in the latest conference, that he has started attending Chinese school every Sunday, where he is learning to read and write Cantonese. Wing has brought some of his Cantonese work into school and from the silent child at the age of 3, he has developed into an expert in his class, explaining to his teacher and to the other children about his knowledge of Cantonese. In part this change has been brought about by his teachers demonstrating through the use of the conferences, that they really want to know about Wing's knowledge and experiences from home. His teachers have made it clear that his bilingualism is valued and respected and that school can be a safe place for him to explore talking, reading and writing. It is significant that Margaret noted on his PLR summary sheet in Spring 1991:

> Wing is exceptionally vocal when in the role play areas, such as the house, or with sand and water.

In these situations there is no pressure and he can play with language.

The parent and child conferences mean that the voices of parents and children are an important part of the child's official school record. This in turn means that teachers have to take their contributions seriously. We have both found that conferencing has led to exchanges of information and views becoming a part of the whole school year, not just twice yearly when the official conferences take place. As teachers we have a much clearer picture of children and can build on that. We are also learning what children's development looks like over time, as we now have children's Records over several years, and can see patterns emerging. Parents know that they are more likely to be listened to, because the conferences have formalised the fact that teachers value the knowledge parents have about their children.

Equally, through the record-keeping and reporting that forms the rest of the PLR, parents can see the work that teachers are doing to foster their child's literacy development. A clear message is given to children that their views on themselves as learners are valued by parents and teachers and that children's interests can be built on rather than ignored. We believe that this can only contribute to improved relations, both between schools and parents, and between teachers and children.

References

Barrs, M. et al. (1988) *Primary Language Record*, London: Centre for Language in Primary Education.

Barrs, M. et al. (1988) *Primary Language Record Handbook*, London: Centre for Language in Primary Education.

Clark, M. (1976) *Young Fluent Readers*, London: Heinemann.

In the history of most literate societies there is a period when compulsory education begins with a unified system of instruction dependent on formal classroom discipline and set exercises. Only lately have the different learning styles of individual children come to the fore as one of the reasons for different rates of progress. It has also taken a long time for parents, the literates of an earlier generation, to be persuaded that there is no single way to teach reading and writing that will guarantee success. Those who have had very little experience of literacy for themselves, or whose encounters with the powerful literates of their community have not been reassuring, sometimes expect that when their children learn to read they will immediately enter the world of the learned. It is also difficult for them to believe that activities such as making dolls, play-acting and reading folk tales have significant consequences for reading and writing.

The children in this study are older than others in this book. But their case-study reinforces what has emerged from each chapter: how the teachers' insights, care and understanding of the wider implications of literacy make the learners' view of their task more relevant, hopeful and fulfilling. It is significant that we should conclude these studies with a piece from Greece, the culture to which many countries owe their alphabet and their appreciation of literature and dramatic art.

Chapter 7

MAKING OLD TOYS TOGETHER: PARENTS AND CHILDREN CREATE A NEW PURPOSE FOR LITERACY LEARNING IN ATHENS

Aris Sioutis and Poppy Kyrdi

Aris writes:

Firmly imprinted in my memory is the anxiety of a mother bringing her child to Primary One for the first time, and asking me: 'How will my little boy manage to learn to read and write?' This anxiety would not have been of any great significance if the child, Dimitris, had not already manifested major difficulties in reading and writing. And Dimitris was not the only one; there were also Yhta, Yiannis, Achilleas..........

This was the school year 1989-90, when I first started working at Vyronas 2nd Primary School, an educational establishment numbering 20 teachers and approximately 350 pupils. The school is in Vyronas, a working and lower middle class suburb of Athens, and is set amidst the old quarries and little houses of a former refugee settlement.

The school building is of the standard type, and uninspiring. The classrooms, which are cold and impersonal, are also used by the area's high school students. The children cannot arrange the classrooms and their desks as they would like, nor put up their work for display: they often find their work has been destroyed.

My previous experience — two years in a school on the small island of Sifnos — was quite different: there I was the only teacher and was required to teach all levels of pupils. Thus, when I took up my new post at Vyronas as a teacher of Primary One pupils, I had one thought uppermost in my mind: how would I be able to meet the demands and needs of each child?

My acquaintance with Lefteris, a child in Primary Six at this school, played an important role at that time. I had been introduced to him by the teacher of special education, in order to give him some extra help at home. He was having particular difficulties in reading and writing, and of the four principles of arithmetic he knew only addition. More important however, was the opinion which the school had formed of this boy: he was considered to be a student with aggressive tendencies, lazy, and of low intellectual ability. His teacher had summed him up by saying: 'You'll just be wasting your time. Lefteris won't learn anything.'

In due course the school authorities were to be proved wrong. Lefteris learned all four principles of arithmetic, using decimals and fractions. I also discovered that he was able to mend several household appliances that were out of order at home, and he could spend hours making a new bicycle out of parts from old ones. I did not use any special methods (which in any case I did not know) with Lefteris. The whole thing was based on our relationship. I accepted him as he was. I understood his difficulties and we set out together to try and overcome them. I speculated a great deal on the change in Lefteris, and it caused me to rethink the manner in which I worked at school.

There was another factor which had contributed to this change in Lefteris: his participation in a theatre group. Pupils from Primary Five and Primary Six at our school who had reading and writing difficulties used to collaborate with a team from the University in putting on a play. Lefteris asked me to help him learn his part. We went to rehearsals together, and there I met Poppy Kyrdi and Z. Mouratian, two postgraduate students with scholarships to the University's Department of Education. A little while later, while accompanying the children to the radio station where they were to present their play, I also made the acquaintance of Mrs. Varnava Skouras, a lecturer at the University.

Urged on by them, I decided to continue my studies in the University of Athens Department of Education while at the same time working at the school.

Poppy writes:

I came to know Aris and his class through the action research project on the prevention of functional illiteracy in basic education, carried out during the school years 1988-90 in schools in Vyronas by a team from the University in which I took part, under the direction of Mrs. Tzela Varnava-Skouras.

We concentrated our intervention on activities aimed at providing support for pupils in Primary Five and later Primary Six (aged 11-12 years). We restricted ourselves to the processes of diagnosing the perception children have of the relationship between the written and the spoken word (Ferreiro and Teberosky 1979) and through these procedures to identifying those children with difficulties in learning the first stages of reading and writing.

As a young teacher, Aris devoted a great deal of time to his students outside school hours. We noticed that he tried to help weak students in their integration into the class and in their attempts to learn to read and write, assuming that these children were no less clever than their peers but that their difficulties were due to social and psychological factors. He never called them poor students and he made frequent efforts to approach them. The number of these children was by no means negligible: five or six out of a total of 22; in other words, one quarter of the class. His sensitivity, his pleasure each time a child made a step towards attaining the knowledge offered to him, his fighting spirit, his anxiety to discover new methods in the teaching process and to broaden the children's interests were the reasons for embarking on a joint project in 1989 that is still going on today.'

The Greek education system has a rigid structure which does not easily accommodate new ideas. Daily educational practice is determined by a full, detailed and unified syllabus and timetable which renders the handling of any subject-matter outside the schedule almost impossible, even if it has the same aims as those of the syllabus. Whether they live in a rural or urban part of the country, all Greek children use the same textbooks and are taught the same things at more or less the same time (Gotovos 1986). Schools therefore have to be selective (Frangoudaki 1985). The teachers who work in Greek Primary Schools at present undergo a brief two year period of teacher training. Further training is rare and largely a matter of luck or individual persistence.

The closed structure of the Greek education system, the traditionally teacher-oriented method of instruction, and the strict civil service hierarchy, act as a brake on any kind of initiative (Gotovos et al. 1985). Every school day closely resembles the day before or the day after, and the teachers and children keep to the lesson schedule because they are obliged to do so. During a lesson the school classroom is a taboo area in which nobody apart from the teacher and the children is permitted, except for occasional visits by the headmaster or the education advisor, to observe or, even more rarely, to participate in the daily education process. A Ministry ot Education circular specifies this.

Emboldened by our collaboration, in the autumn of 1990 we drew up a plan of alternative classroom activities based on the children's interests and aimed at improving reading and writing skills. Our basic standpoint was that children participate and enjoy writing when it has a purpose, when it is directed towards a particular reader, and is connected with things they like doing best (Varnava-Skouras 1990). We therefore developed our activities around the theme of play: its history, its structure, the ways in which it is carried out. At the same time we also endeavoured to promote the idea of recycling materials, since, on Aris's initiative, the school had already embarked on such a programme.

We attempted to involve parents in our plan because we believe in the reinforcing role of the child's co-operation with his family, and also because we wanted to improve the contact between parents and children. The difficulties we encountered in parental participation h the activities of the class were as follows:

(1) the prohibiting by the educational hierarchy of 'strangers' in the classroom:

(2) the parents' employment and their reservations;

(3) the fact that co-operation between older and younger members is not common practice in the Greek family.

Our efforts met with obstruction from the other teachers and the headmaster, as our activities fell outside the syllabus and therefore seemed doomed to failure from the outset. Despite the adverse conditions we went ahead with our plan, using the hours normally taken up with lessons in aesthetic education and the study of the environment.

The first activity took place in December 1990. The children made objects in class out of various 'useless' materials (rags, tin cans, plastic bottles, pieces of wood and paper, all used) which they brought from home. Articles which had been destined for the rubbish-bin were turned into Santa Clauses, little cars, rockets, vases and pencil cases. We decided, with the children, to package their work in paper bags so that they could exchange presents at Christmas.

Unfortunately the reaction of the parents was not always positive. Having been through periods when they were deprived of basic goods, they subconsciously see the possession and use of a rubbish-bin as a sign of affluence and dismiss as valueless anything that is derived from rubbish. For this reason Vasso's mother did not allow her daughter to put the doll she had made on her desk as she considered it to be cheap and nasty.

Our next step was to hold a discussion in class about the importance of and need for recycling. This resulted in the production of a small written questionnaire. The children were to collect information about the packaging and use of various products in the old days by asking their parents and grandparents. In this way the family also became involved in our 'game'.

This time parents and grandparents responded positively to the idea and were pleased to answer the children's questions. All the children, even those who usually had difficulty in writing and rarely did their normal written homework for school, enjoyed bringing back the answers they had collected, reading them and exchanging information with each other.
Klio wrote:

'My parents told me that when they were young they didn't throw things away in the rubbish. They found lots of other uses for them; they put sugar, coffee or sweets into glass jars. Empty bottles were used for olive oil, paraffin and different sorts of drinks which they made themselves.'

Others painted similar pictures:

'My mother said they had very little rubbish in those days. They used to keep old newspapers and paper to wrap up presents and sweets' (Maria).

They embroidered the sacks that peas and beans were stored in and made rugs out of them. Milk tins were opened at one end and drunk out of, and then they were used to make coffee in or as saucepans' (Andreas).

My grandmother told me they used to keep gold jewellery, pins or nails in old tins' (Achilleas).

'My grandfather said they used to use old newspapers as toilet paper (Iannis).

Using their imagination and their own recent experiences, the children were then asked to write about The Adventures of a Paper Bag, a Bottle or a Tin Can.

'The Story of a Tin Can' by Vicky

'I am a very pretty tin can. But now I'm going to tell you my own story. Well, one day I was bought at the supermarket and I had one sardine in me. The people took me home and emptied the smelly fish out of me and I felt better. The next day washed me well and then put a lovely, delicious sweet inside me. As soon as the people had eaten the sweet, they threw me in the rubbish-bin along with some other things. Gradually I got crushed, and the children felt sorry for me and took me out of the rubbish. Well, these children put a hat on me and made me into a doll. But I still got crushed, so that was the end of me.'

Working together with the parents this time, we made up some games in the classroom which they used to play when they were little. This gave us the idea of finding out about traditional 'folk' games, starting with team games which were played in open spaces.

Our proposal was received with enthusiasm by both parents and children. We met in the school playground during the last two hours one Friday. The ten mothers who came were asked not just

Figure 25: 'A father making a traditional windmill with eager helpers'

to learn but also to play two team games from their childhood with the children. After an initial period of awkwardness, the oldest of the mothers began to show the children the first game called Chuck-Stone which is rather like the English Five-Stones. Seven year old Klio and her mother explain how it is played.

'You play the game with five small almond-shaped stones. You put them on a table, then pick one up and throw it up, trying at the same time to grab one of the other stones left on the table and then catch the first stone as it comes down. If you drop either stone you are out, but if you catch both, you put one aside and carry on, throwing up the first stone and picking up the others in turn. If you manage to pick up all the stones without dropping one, you start again, this time picking the stones up in twos. And if you manage this, you try to pick up three at once, and then four. If you succeed, you then move on to the second pan of the game. For this you cross the index finger of your left hand over the third finger and make an arch, with you thumb touching the table. with your right hand you put the five

109

stones in front of the arch, then pick one up, throw it up high, and at the same time push one of the stones left on the table through the arch, and catch the first stone as it comes down. You carry on until you have pushed all the stones through the arch. There are many further variations, but the winner is always the one who has gone through all the steps without dropping a stone.

Their gaiety communicated itself to other mothers and soon parents and children were playing together. There was tremendous enthusiasm, and one mother said as she was leaving: 'I really enjoyed myself because it took me back to my childhood'. Only two mothers did not take part because they thought the games were childish.

Other such meetings took place. The children kept a record of how the games were played and presented them in a special performance organised by the Parents Association of the school as part of the Vyronas Municipality's Children's Festival.

The children's interest in school has apparently increased as a result of these activities. Even children with reading and writing difficulties are unwilling to lose a day's school. Once when Iota, a girl with problems in reading and writing, was unwell, her mother thought it quite natural that she should stay at home. To her surprise she found that Iota had got up before her, had got herself ready for school and then made her mother take her to school.

In an effort to find ways in which Dimitris would be able to respond to the programme, Aris visited the boy's home:

'His parents did not participate in the activities we organised at school. Their awareness of belonging to a low social class, the difficult conditions under which they lived and the poor performance of their child had made them diffident and insecure. This insecurity was very marked in Dimitris. My interest in the child was much appreciated by the parents, and a relationship grew up between us based on trust and mutual understanding. This relationship was a great help in getting the boy to participate in the life of the class.'

The pleasure experienced by the children, the positive response of the pupils who had reading and writing difficulties and the interest of the parents prompted Aris to ask the headmaster if an exception could be made in his case, so that he would be allowed to keep the same class for the third successive year, in order to continue the activities centring on play.

We had a meeting in September 1991 to consider the schedule for the new school year. Armed with the support of the parents and also the experience we had gained during the previous school year, the results of which we deemed to be very positive, we set our aims with greater certainty. These were:

- to support the positive relationship with the parents by encouraging them to take part in the life of the class and by helping them to understand the importance of their participation in their children's education;

- to carry on with our activities based on play, by looking at the evolution of play and continuing to make thing s from recycled 'useless' materials;

- to spark off the children's interest in writing through these activities.

In order to realise the first of these goals, we asked parents to suggest topics that they would be interested in discussing at our regular monthly meetings, which up to now had served merely as occasions for us to provide the parents with an official report on their children's progress. Great interest was shown in this proposal, but there were also reservations: 'Nice idea, but these things seldom get off the ground.' The first of these discussions, dealing with the subject of 'The Family and the Development of the Child' has already taken place.

To meet our second aim, we sought the help of museums, organisations and individuals who could provide us with appropriate material. We borrowed from the Museum of Cycladic Art and the Benaki Museum some museum kits entitled: 'Play in Ancient Greece' and 'Popular Greek Folk Games'. In re-enacting and playing the games of their parents and grandparents, the children were surprised and pleased to discover that many of them were similar to present-day games. Their interest in the history and evolution of play had been stimulated. Indeed, the popular traditional dolls excited so much interest that the children asked to learn how to make them, and this resulted in the organisation of our first activity this year involving the participation of the parents, on the making of traditional dolls.

For two hours the classroom became a hive of activity. After one of the mothers had demonstrated how to make the doll, the twelve

Figure 26: 'Parents and children making traditional dolls'

parents and 22 children divided themselves into groups and set to
work, using old clothes, used paper and bottles, pieces of wood and
paints. In some groups the children showed as much initiative as
the parents; in others, it was the parents who led the way. The
children were completely absorbed in their work and for the first
time in the three years they had been at the school they did not want
to go out at break-time. When they had finished, they wrote a brief
report indicating the name of their doll and the method and
materials they had used in her construction. A photograph of their
work was later added to the file. Parents and children alike — even
Vasso's mother — left the classroom proudly clutching their dolls
and asking for this co-operation to continue.

The first step had been taken: the majority of the parents had
been not merely convinced of the value of their participation in the
class's activities, but were positively enthusiastic about it.

In seeking to attain our third goal, we then asked the children to
share their experience with the pupils in another school by writing
to them about our school and the objects we had made, and giving

Figure 27: 'Writing instructions for making the dolls'

them written instructions in how to make the dolls. The children were enthusiastic about the idea and brought envelopes and stamps to school, asking to know the names of their respective pen-friends. These are the pupils in Primary Two (one year below them) of a private school, whose teacher, Dimitra Cosmopoulou, had been a member of the University research team.

For the children, the task of writing now has a specific aim and has therefore become a tool of communication and won the children's interest. By writing they will acquire new friends in another area and a different environment, and they will have something to 'teach' these new friends. The pupils with reading and writing difficulties, who also want to have their own pen-friend, make the effort to write because they feel that this time the exercise has a purpose.

The pen-friend project was a good opportunity for Aris to get closer to the children with reading and writing difficulties and their families. He visited their homes to discuss with the parents the aims of the project and the ways in which we could help the children. He suggested that the children should come to school for two hours a week outside the normal school hours to work on the project. We were thus able to provide support teaching with the co-operation of the parents and in a manner that was painless and free of stress for the children.

One of the homes which Aris visited was that of Akis. Aris writes:

'When Akis first came to our school at the end of Primary Two, he was still unable to read or write. His family had moved house frequently and Akis had already changed schools three times. His grandmother used to bring him to school every day. I asked to see his parents so that we could have a talk. A woman came to one of our Parents' meetings and Akis told me that she was his mother. However, a month later another woman came to see me at the school and said *she* was his mother and that she could not come regularly because she worked as a 'singer'. I was unable to meet his father. From a recent discussion which I had with Akis's grandmother and mother at their home, I realised that despite their good intentions, the mother's night-time occupation, her constant absence from the home, their poor living conditions and low levels of education, made it practically impossible for Akis to get any help at home.'

Yet Akis is very keen to acquire a new friend through the pen-pal scheme:

'My friend Stavros, I go to school near the Vyronas quarries. My name is Akis. We made some dolls in our class. I made one out of a tin can with a sock and it has a hat...' (Excerpt from his letter).

Our perseverance with these activities has begun to have an effect on the whole climate at our school. The Primary Two teacher, Sophia Stranga, has already shown an interest in carrying out similar activities with her class. When a new circular about environmental education arrived from the Ministry of Education, we got together and drew up plans for the future, using the environmental studies lesson.

The aim of our activities is to create a link between the school and environmental protection, Greek folk traditions in a modern setting and the family, within a framework that goes beyond the formal school timetable and stimulates a positive attitude on the part of the children towards knowledge and school. Against this background, writing is seen as a means of communication, a tool which has a much wider use than merely doing school lessons.

114

References

Ferreiro, E. E. and Teberosky, A. (1979) *Literacy Before Schooling*. New York: Heinemann:

Folerou, F. E. and Freiderikou, A. (1991) *Daskali Tou Dimotikou Sholiou, Mia Kinoniologiki Prossegissi*. Athens: Ypsilon

Frangoudaki, A. (1985) 'I anisotita sto eliniko sholio' in *Kinoniologia Tis Ekpedefsis*. Athens: Papazissis

Gotovos, A. (1986) *I Logiki Tou Yparktou Sholiou*. Athens: Synchroni Ekpedefsi:

Gotovos, A., Marrogiorgos, G. E. and Papa Konstantinou (1985) *Kritiki Pedagogiki ke Ekpedeftiki Praxi* Athens: Synchroni Edpedifsi

AFTERWORD

In all their variety, the accounts in these pages show us how early literacy learning can be enriching and enlarging for all concerned — parents and teachers as well as children. They show us that where literacy learning is engaged in as an extension of the business of giving meaning and order both to the outside world and to the inner world of the imagination, all those involved develop a stronger sense of who they are and of what these worlds have to offer them.

The partnerships we have been shown are paradigmatic instances, sensitively construed, of interventions between parents and children, parents and teachers, and teachers and other professionals in the wider domain of education. They have been brought about by the willingness of each to encounter the other and the results show a growth of mutual understanding, common interests and confidence, all of which is reflected in the children's learning.

But these are only beginnings. Now we see the need for two kinds of development. First there is a need for further action research. As educators we are bound to ask ourselves where our next steps should take our various European initiatives. We have recorded common concerns: we know the desire of parents to understand better how children learn in school so that they can be more helpful at home. But sharing one another's perceptions is not always easy. Where a mother sees little value in her child's early writing, there is still much explaining to do amongst all those concerned for the child's growth in literacy.

117

How, then, can we help such partnerships forward? What should we usefully tell parents in the different cultural contexts of schooling? Academics know that the evidence they need for good research into children's development is first visible in the classroom interactions between teachers and pupils. How are good collaborative endeavours sustained by the education authorities in schools and universities? What kinds of books, other texts and information technology promote literacy learning after children have become fluent and confident readers and writers? Questions such as these demand to be explored.

In each of our countries there are reservoirs of research, abundant goodwill to share it, economic imperatives to promote it. How then can we go beyond the confines of bureaucratic restraints — governmental, linguistic and monetary — to promote our concern for the potential of all children in a changing Europe?

Perhaps we should and can continue where we have begun: with the children themselves. We need to know more about how the children we want to help, understand the learning tasks we want them to encompass. So we shall continue to seek common understandings and appreciate cultural difficulties, the better to refine our practices.

But research on its own cannot be enough. We also need to ensure that the collaborations reported here spread wide to encompass all the children of Europe, not just a favoured few. To do this we must recognise and provide the conditions that allow such fruitful interactions. Collaborative partnerships do not arise by chance: they need to be developed with care and patience, in institutional settings that provide sensitive recognition of the cultures in which they are embedded. The various countries of Europe make very differing provision for young children and recognise in varying degrees the role parents have to play in their formal education. We consider that all countries should, at the very least, provide:

- respect for parents as the first and most important educators of their children;

- nursery schooling for all children over three years whose parents wish it;

- recognition that teachers in nursery school and the early years of primary school require as much training as their

118

colleagues elsewhere in the school system, and should be similarly rewarded;

- substantial pre-service and in-service training for teachers of young children, both in the part parents can play in their children's learning and in the importance of cultural differences, particularly with respect to literacy;

- formal recognition of the educative role of parents through provision for their involvement as educators in school activities, and of a framework for substantial home-school dialogue;

- opportunities for teachers and schools to make innovations of the kind presented in this book and to share these with colleagues.

At the moment we are seeing interesting developments in many different parts of Europe. Now we need to use our growing European identity to share and extend these developments so that all our children, including particularly those from minority cultures, may start their formal education without feeling that they are entering a strange and alien world. In our increasingly multicultural communities, collaboration between teachers and parents in helping young children make sense of the literacies around them can be a powerful means of bringing people together.